D0563321

Capturing
Enigma

Capturing Enigma

How HMS *Petard* Seized the German Naval Codes

Stephen Harper

The History Press

This book was first published in 1999 by
Sutton Publishing Limited

First published in this edition in 2002 by
Sutton Publishing Limited

Reprinted in 2008 by The History Press

Copyright © Stephen Harper, 2008

All rights reserved. No part of this publication may be
reproduced, stored in a retrieval syatem, or transmitted,
in any form, or by any means, electronic, mechanical,
photocopying, recording or otherwise, without the prior
permission of the publisher and copyright holder.

Stephen Harper has asserted the moral right to be
identified as the author of this work.

British Library Cataloguing in Publication Data
A catalogue record for this book is available from the
British Library.

ISBN 978 0 7509 3050 5

Typeset in 10/12pt Sabon.
Typesetting and origination by
Sutton Publishing Limited.
Printed and bound in England by
Ashford Colour Press Ltd, Gosport, Hampshire.

In memory of the men who sacrificed their lives to capture the Enigma documents:

Lt Anthony Fasson RN, George Cross
AB Colin Grazier, George Cross
and their companion
NAAFI assistant Tom Brown, George Medal

Contents

Preface

The fighting record of the Royal Navy fleet destroyer HMS *Petard* was unique in the Second World War. She was the only warship of any Allied navy to sink a submarine of all three enemy navies. She was also a survivor of Malta convoys and of the disastrous Aegean campaign that became known as the destroyers' graveyard. But by far her greatest coup remained a top secret for so long that the name HMS *Petard* is still little known.

The enormous consequences of HMS *Petard*'s action coming up to 60 years ago, against a German U-boat in the Eastern Mediterranean, far from the dominating Atlantic struggle could well have put the ship's name almost on a par with Nelson's Victory had it been possible to release the facts of her triumph at the time. The strategic consequences of Nelson's victory at Tralfagar ended Napoleon's dream of crossing the channel and made the Royal Navy undisputed master of the seas and oceans. The consequences of HMS *Petard*'s success, which cost the lives of two of her crew, were just as significant.

The capture of key coding material for a modified German Enigma coding machine that had defied all British efforts to decode it during a critical ten months of 1942 was the crucial factor in defeating the U-boat wolf packs when they were on the brink of triumph in the

Atlantic. The U-boat offensive came close to preventing the build-up of US forces for the 1944 invasion of fortress Europe and to achieving Germany's aim in two world wars of starving Britain into seeking an armistice, and came close to preventing the build-up of United States forces for the 1944 invasion of Hitler's Fortress Europe.

The Battle of the Atlantic was the key campaign, the longest and most important struggle of the Second World War. Winston Churchill said it was the dominating factor throughout the war. If it had been lost no other triumphs would have counted.

An extended intelligence black-out lasting nearly four decades ensured that the destroyer HMS *Petard*'s achievement remained unknown, her fame unrecognised. Few had heard of her save for former crew members and members of the secret establishment at Bletchley Park decoding headquarters in Buckinghamshire.

There at last the Bletchley Park Trust has put on public display part of the story that reveals the nation's debt to a warship that fame passed by, a warship surely worthy of a place alongside Nelson's *Victory* in Portsmouth dockyard. Sadly HMS *Petard* was broken up for scrap in 1967, some 25 years after her launch into the River Tyne.

In fact there is a historic link between the *Petard*'s action on 30 October 1942 and Nelson's victory at Trafalgar. The author learned of this only after publication of the hardback edition of this book. The sister of Lieutenant Anthony Fasson, who swam with Able Seaman Colin Grazier to seize the documents before the U-boat sank, wrote to correct the spelling of her brother's first name, wrongly spelt Antony in official documents. She also told the author that Anthony was the fifth generation of her family to have served in the Royal Navy, a descendant of the captain of HMS *Swiftsure* at Trafalgar.

[There is a current campaign to save the only surviving wartime destroyer, HMS *Cavalier*, and maintain her in the historic dockyard at Chatham.]

The author had a personal interest in HMS *Petard*, having lived aboard her as a coder during her second commission with the East Indies Fleet at the end of the war against Japan. At that time I knew nothing of my ship's glorious first commission, hearing of her distinction as the only Allied ship to sink submarines of all three enemy navies from a book of photographs of wartime ships a few years ago. Soon afterwards, in February 1994, I read in *The Times* of the controversial depth charging of a Japanese super-submarine by the *Petard* after the sinking of the troopship *Khedive Ismail* while survivors were in the water – another action kept top secret for many years.

It was not until March 1997 that I read a brief mention of the *Petard*'s capture of the Enigma material in a *Times* obituary for Capt A.J. Baker Cresswell, captain of the destroyer *Bulldog* during the capture of earlier Enigma material from a U-boat in the Atlantic in May 1941. That really stimulated my interest. I read every document mentioning HMS *Petard* at the Public Record Office. There was much material on the sinking of the Italian and Japanese submarines but nothing at all about the sinking of the *U-559*. After I asked why this was, some documents about it have become available there.

While seeking members of the *Petard*'s first commission crew for eyewitness accounts I discovered that an account of the first commission had been written by the former gunnery officer, G.G. Connell, in 1976. In a 1994 edition of his book, aptly titled *Fighting Destroyer*, Connell added a paragraph saying that at the time of writing he had had no idea of the priceless value of the material recovered from the *U-559*. He was already ill, and died shortly afterwards.

It was clear that the full story of this unique warship and the immense consequences of the action in which two crew members gave their lives had still to be told. My thanks go to Reg Crang, secretary of the HMS *Petard* Association, for free use of quotations from his graphic diary; Lt Cdr Robert de Pass RN, a former first lieutenant of the *Petard*, for free use of pictures he took in the thick of action; John Mackness, one of *Petard*'s oerlikon gunners; Jack Hall, one of the Asdic operators; Stan Reynolds, who was in the whaler that carried the invaluable Enigma material captured from *U-559* back to the *Petard*; Mervyn Romeril, a former bridge lookout; Ted Saunders, a former leading seaman, and to all veterans of the fighting first commission. To Lieut. Fasson's sister, Mrs Sheena d'Anyers Willis, for his naval family background. Also to Peter Allen, a second commission telegraphist, and Les Turnham who served in the *Petard* after the war when she was converted to a frigate.

Ralph Erskine, a top authority on naval signals intelligence, kindly checked and suggested amendments to the Enigma passages; Mrs Joan Connell gave permission for the use of direct quotes from her late husband's book; Dr John Horsey advised me of the existence of the HMS *Petard* Association; former Major Robert Findlay checked the account of the Salerno invasion; former merchant navy chief engineer Ian Blair helped research into the Battle of the Atlantic; Terry Fincher helped with photographs, and my wife Mary with copy reading.

Thanks also to John Gallehawk and others at the Bletchley Park Museum, and to the staffs of the Public Record Office, the Imperial War Museum and the British Library.

Part One
The Enigma Story

Chapter One
The Secret that Won the War

German intelligence never found out that two British sailors from the destroyer HMS *Petard* gave their lives while searching a sinking U-boat abandoned by her crew, and passing keys to breaking the German Navy's top secret Enigma cipher to shipmates. Their exploit was one of the most sensitive secrets of the Second World War, and was kept secret for nearly forty years afterwards. It was perhaps the most important single exploit of the whole war. The material they died in obtaining was to have enormous consequences, though they could not have known just how important a prize they were passing up the conning tower in their last moments in the enemy craft that was to be their tomb. The captured material was precious beyond evaluation. It enabled cryptanalysts at Bletchley Park, the ultra-secret Government Cipher and Code School, to break the four-rotor systems of the ingenious German Enigma cipher machine, thought by the German High Command to make their U-boat signals impossible to decode.

Earlier in the war Bletchley Park, building on Polish achievments, had succeeded in breaking into the earlier German Enigma machine which used three rotors, but the code-breakers had been stumped when the Germans added a fourth rotor for the use of U-boats in the Atlantic and Mediterranean in February 1942 in readiness for an all-out U-boat offensive aimed at cutting Britain's Atlantic lifelines once and for all. This had blacked out vital intelligence about U-boat operations for almost ten critical months, and the *Petard*'s coup came just in time for Bletchley Park to solve the four-rotor systems and provide the intelligence that gave the Allied navies the upper hand in the most critical phase of the Atlantic battle in the spring of 1943.

Had they continued to be in the dark about the contents of U-boat traffic, the Allies would have been unable to establish naval supremacy in the Atlantic until the second half of 1943 at the earliest, and the invasion of Europe would probably have been delayed until 1945 or later.

This key Allied success began soon after the destroyer HMS *Petard* began operations in the eastern Mediterranean, far from the Atlantic struggle that her action was to influence so greatly. On 30 October 1942, after a day-long hunt, the *Petard*'s depth charges forced the *U-559* to the surface in darkness some sixty miles north of Port Said, and her crew began to abandon her.

Without waiting for a boat to be lowered Lt Antony Fasson and AB Colin Grazier stripped naked and swam through water swarming with the rescue-seeking German crew to reach the U-boat. They were followed aboard by a sixteen-year-old NAAFI assistant, Tommy Brown, who jumped onto the U-boat when the *Petard* moved briefly alongside. He then joined them inside the U-boat and made three trips, carrying books and documents found by Fasson and Grazier, back up the conning tower ladder to hand to a boarding party that had come alongside in one of the ship's boats.

Fasson and Grazier died when a rush of water down the conning tower entombed them as the U-boat suddenly went down while they were trying to pass up what they probably thought was a secret coding machine; Brown and others were picked out of the water.

The *Petard*'s crew, stunned by the loss of their shipmates, had no idea of the importance of this tragic incident. The capture of the material was so hush-hush that even the posthumous decorations Fasson and Grazier were awarded had to be disguised to ensure their exploit did not arouse German curiosity. Instead of the Victoria Cross, the top gallantry award they so surely merited, their relatives were presented with the George Cross, normally awarded for the highest gallantry by civilians in air raids. This award had also gone to servicemen for bravery in defusing magnetic mines and unexploded bombs. Tommy Brown was awarded the George Medal, another award usually made to civilians.

The bereaved families of Fasson and Grazier remained mystified, knowing nothing of the circumstances of their deaths. The Admiralty's reasoning in not recommending the highest bravery decoration was on the slim pretence that the VC was intended for the bravest deeds carried out in the face of the enemy and this action was carried out after fighting had stopped. The real reason was that the Admiralty feared that the award of the top military award might alert German intelligence into finding out what lay behind the deaths of the two Navy men. The nightmare for the Admiralty, as well as for Bletchley Park, was that even German suspicion of what had happened was likely to bring about another change in the Enigma code that had eluded solution for so long.

Almost a year after the action the *London Gazette* announced in September 1943 the posthumous awards of the George Cross to Lt Antony Blair Fasson and AB Colin Grazier for 'outstanding bravery and steadfast devotion to duty in the face of danger', but gave no other details. It also announced the award of the George Medal to junior canteen assistant Thomas William Brown for 'bravery and devotion to duty in the face of danger'. Lt Fasson's name is among those on the war memorial at Jedburgh Abbey. His George Cross is exhibited in Edinburgh Castle.

But there were no headlines to cheer the British people through this period of successive defeats and setbacks. Because of its momentous repercussions *Petard*'s triumph had to remain one of the best kept secrets of the war.

The Admiralty had used the prefix Hydro on intelligence based on material from deciphered messages sent on an earlier system for U-boats called Hydra. Ultra, meaning Ultra Secret, was adopted for top intelligence sent to all British services in 1943. It was the code-word prefix for enemy intelligence gathered from ciphers using all types of the ingenious German Enigma machine and all other high-grade signals intelligence.

Distribution was limited to members of the War Cabinet, the most senior advisers and military chiefs Ultra messages were so secret that use of its information in countering enemy action was sometimes disallowed for fear of the Germans realising their 'unbreakable codes' had been broken. Its security rating was as high as that for the atomic bomb, and the only espionage leak from Bletchley Park was also for the use of Moscow. Carefully edited intelligence on German plans was made available to Britain's allies, but John Cairncross, one of the Cambridge spies, who worked at Bletchley Park as a German translator, admitted in a recent autobiography that he gave Bletchley Park material about German intentions on the Russian front to his KGB controllers (see Epilogue). Thousands of people working at Bletchley Park and hundreds more in its associated outposts (and later a few score in the United States), had limited 'need to know' knowledge of what Ultra was about. All were sworn to total secrecy. And the secrecy preserved was extraordinary. Cairncross apart, there were no leaks, no mentions in memoirs. Wives and families could be told nothing about the work their husbands or other relatives did. Secrecy has never been more rigorously applied. Churchill called the Bletchley Park staff 'The geese that laid the golden eggs but never cackled.'

Bletchley Park's work was crucial in saving Britain from early defeat and eventually in winning the war, particularly in bringing victory in 1945 instead of, perhaps, two years later. The huts where decrypters and analysts worked night and day were protected by blast walls and key machinery was operated in concrete bunkers, but the Luftwaffe never raided it. Only one bomb fell just inside the grounds, during a raid on a nearby railway works.

The work at Bletchley Park was such a heavily guarded secret that operations there remained officially unmentionable not only during the war, but also for the first three decades of peace. Even today, when Bletchley Park is open to the public on alternate weekends, disclosure of details about some methods of obtaining intelligence is still under strict wraps.

Until 1974 any and all open reference to Ultra was banned. That year the retired intelligence chief in charge of the dissemination of Ultra intelligence, Wg Cdr Fred Winterbotham, was allowed to publish a discreet book called *The Ultra Secret*, written from his own recollections and without access to documents. Even now, after more than fifty years, some aspects are still secret.

The official ban on any reference to Ultra through all those years, a time when so many books about the war were published, has been a great inhibition to military historians. Most of the books published before 1974, including official histories, are now outdated and many accounts of battles and campaigns need reappraisal. We now know that military commanders had fairly full knowledge of the German command's strength and intentions when they made their own plans.

In 1977 a large number of actual Ultra signals were released at last to the Public Record Office in Kew, and this sparked the publication of several other books, all written without knowledge of the role played by HMS *Petard*. At that time, too, HMS *Petard*'s former gunnery officer, G.G. Connell, wrote *Fighting Destroyer* about the actions in which his ship took part, but at the time of writing he knew nothing of the immense value of the items captured from the *U-559*, or of the significant consequences.

Study of the *Petard* material at Bletchley Park during the winter of 1942 ended a critical lack of intelligence about U-boat movements and operations that had lasted nearly ten months. It came at a time when U-boats were sinking merchant ships twice as fast as new ships were being built, threatening to starve Britons already on meagre rations, and were also hindering the steady build-up of troops, weaponry and equipment for the invasion of Germany's 'fortress Europe'.

Ralph Erskine, an authority on naval signals intelligence, revealed in a letter to *The Times* of 18 March 1997, that the three *Petard* crew members had secured two important code books used by U-boats. He added 'From December 1942 to June 1942, these were the only means by which Bletchley Park could find "cribs" (probable wording of signals) with which to break the Shark – Bletchley Park's name for a new German cipher used by Atlantic U-boats. This helped turn the course of the war, and played a major part in winning the war. Few acts of courage by three individuals can ever had such far reaching consequences.' This echoed an Intelligence and National Security report he wrote in 1988 which stated:

> Without special intelligence from Triton (the four-rotor Enigma system) the U-boats would still have been defeated in the long run, but the cost in human life in the global conflict at large would have been even more terrible than it was. Without the breaking of Shark (Bletchley Park's code name for Triton) the Allies would not have established naval supremacy in the Atlantic until the second half of 1943 at the earliest and the invasion of Europe would probably have been delayed at least until 1945.

With the *Petard* material the four-rotor Enigma U-boat traffic code was broken within six weeks. It resulted in the Admiralty reading vital operational signals between U-boats and the U-boat commander, Adm Karl Doenitz, in time to take countermeasures. Convoys were routed around areas where U-boat wolf-packs lay in ambush, and so many U-boats were sunk after being located by Ultra that Doenitz found his losses unacceptable and ordered his U-boats to leave the North Atlantic for safer waters.

The key Battle of the Atlantic had been a close-run thing. When U-boats operating in the Atlantic increased by a third from January to April 1941, a low point in the Battle of the Atlantic when the German naval Enigma was still secure, Churchill made a sombre broadcast to the nation, telling families clustered around their wireless sets of Britain's dependence on sea traffic, and ending 'When you remember all this, can you wonder that it is the Battle of the Atlantic which holds the first place in the thoughts of those upon whom rests the responsibility for procuring the victory.' After the war Churchill said that the Battle of the Atlantic had been the dominating factor throughout the six years of war, adding

> Never for one moment could we forget that everything that happened elsewhere, on land, at sea, or in the air, depended ultimately on its outcome, and amid all our other cares, we viewed its changing fortunes day by day with hope or apprehension. . . . Amid the torrent of events one anxiety reigned supreme. Battles might be won or lost, enterprises might succeed or miscarry, territoriesmight be gained or quitted, but dominating all our power to carry on the war, or even keep ourselves alive, lay our mastery of the ocean routes and free approach and entry to our ports.

Just how that mastery was finally achieved was Britain's best-kept secret.

Chapter Two

Bletchley Park – the Victory Centre

The ability to read the enemy's most secret communications is a top priority of war. During the First World War a brilliant team of cryptanalysts in Section 25 of naval intelligence, located in Room 40 at the Old Admiralty Building, solved and read 15,000 German coded messages. From October 1914, following the capture of three cipher books, they held the key to the whole German maritime and overseas communications system. One, the cipher used by small ships, Zeppelins and U-boats, was taken by the Australian Navy from a German freighter in the Pacific; the second, a cipher for diplomatic use, was dredged from a wreck in the North Sea; the third came from the German cruiser *Magdeburg* which ran aground in operations against Russia, and the Czarist Navy passed the cipher books on to London. However, this unparalleled advantage was not exploited as it might have been by senior naval officers who had more confidence in signals sent by flag hoist. This system, still used between ships in company, was introduced by Adm Home Popham in time for Nelson to give orders to his fleet at Trafalgar.

Adm William James, who became deputy chief of naval staff in the late 1930s as a new war approached, had been head of naval intelligence when the First World War ended, and he remembered how failure to give proper weight to signal decodes had allowed most of the German High Seas Fleet to escape at the Battle of Jutland. He was determined to ensure full cooperation between intelligence and operations in the coming war, and formed an Operational Intelligence Centre.

Another veteran of Room 40 was Dillwyn Knox, a Greek scholar described as an awesome bridge player, who had remained in government service with the Government Code and Cipher School established in offices on London's Broadway. In the 1930s when the Italian Navy was considered the principal threat, with Mussolini declaring the Mediterranean 'Mare Nostrum', Knox had broken Italian naval ciphers based on a commercial version of the German Enigma. In early 1939 he had also met Polish cryptanalysts who had broken the first German Enigma codes (see Appendix One).

When war came again the official address for the Government Code and Cipher School was Room 47, the Foreign Office. In July 1939 its head, Cdr Alastair Denniston, moved its activities to a Victorian mansion with diverse architectural features, Bletchley Park, set among 56 acres in Buckinghamshire, 50 miles north of London. Its denizens came to know it as BP, but it was also known as Station X after its wireless section. There were outstations in other remote houses scattered around the countryside. Its staff grew from fewer than 100 to nearly 12,000 men and women, with more than 4,000 more working in outstations – all sworn never to reveal anything about their work, even to their families.

In a building in the stable yard behind the mansion, known as 'the cottage', Knox continued his efforts to break the German Enigma (named after the Greek for puzzle) ciphers. He had a considerable kick-start from the study of an Enigma replica made by a Polish firm called AVA, and five rotors, all passed to British intelligence by Polish colleagues a few weeks before war started.

The military Enigma machine weighed 25 lb, was little bulkier than a typewriter and had a similar keyboard except for lacking numbers and ancillary keys. This was connected to a panel of lights. The core of the machine was a cylinder into which three wheels chosen from a set of five (later eight) could be inserted in interchangeable order. Each wheel had twenty-six settings, one for each letter, with a similar number of brass contacts on each side. When a key was pressed the right-hand wheel rotated one notch; after twenty-six movements the middle wheel moved one notch and after twenty-six times twenty-six movements by the right-hand wheel, the left-hand one would rotate by one notch. Under the keyboard, between it and the wheels, a plugboard had twenty-six sockets, with a variable number up to ten holes interlinked by the operator's choice with a plug at each end. At the left of the wheels was a reflector with more cross-connected patterns of letters. The path then traversed the wheels on another path. This arrangement meant that the letter pressed on the keyboard went through seven conversions before it lit up the panel lamp. Movable rings were fitted to the wheels so that the settings themselves were encoded. These electro-mechanical movements provided many millions of possible permutations for each letter.

On Monday 4 September 1939, the day after Britain

declared war, Knox was joined at Bletchley Park by two outstanding Cambridge mathematicians, Alan Turing and Gordon Welchman. They had both been recruited by Cdr Denniston soon after Munich. Alan Turing had earlier won renown for a classic paper on 'computable numbers', recognised as the theoretical basis of modern computers. Welchman combined mathematical genius with a bent for mechanics and organisation.

They quickly recruited scores of the country's leading intellectuals, linguists, chess champions, statisticians and mathematicians. These colleagues made intensive study of intercepted German signals flowing in from the worldwide 'Y' service which listened continuously to all enemy radio networks. Most of the early deciphers came from Luftwaffe traffic whose telegraphists tended to be slapdash, often repeating cipher groups that gave a clue to code settings.

Bletchley's pigeon lofts were extensively used by carrier pigeons, bringing intercepted message from Y branch radio listening stations around the country. People in the small town of Bletchley became used to passing dispatch riders, more than seventy a day entering the Park's heavily guarded gates at the most active stages of the war.

Alan Turing took the tower room across the stable yard to concentrate on breaking the Enigma. Besides the priceless gift of the Polish AVA machine (see Appendix One) they also had blueprints of a pioneering Polish Bomba, code-named after a popular brand of their ice-cream. This was a machine containing the same wiring as the Enigma that would go through all the possible settings. The Poles had begun breaking German Enigma messages after discovering that for the sake of ensuring accuracy the German operators were repeating an initial three-letter setting at the start of every message. So analysis of the opening groups was the way to begin penetrating the system.

Turing called the huge British electromechanical machine, 7 ft wide and 6 ft high, a Bombe. It was made by the British Tabulating Machine Company at nearby Letchworth. They were Enigma machines in reverse, but far more complex. They simulated the three operational rotors of the Enigma thirty-six times, running millions of letters in infinite variations, all aimed at coinciding with a sequence that would decode a German Enigma machine's messages. A 'crib' menu of electromagnetic instructions was set on a plugboard. Sounding like a high-speed knitting machine the Bombe searched the Enigma material fed into it for letter patterns it could not reject as a result of logical testing. When it found one, the machine stopped and the operator, who had no idea what was being looked for, reported success. The menus, used to feed the Bombe, were drawn up by cryptanalysts in Hut 6 based on 'cribs' (probable plain text of the signal) obtained from study of addresses and signatures, repetitions and proliferation of likely Enigma keys. The first Bombe, named Agnes, was operated in Hut 10 from March 1940.

Traffic analysts dealing with German Army and Air Force signals worked in Hut 6 under Gordon Welchman, much helped by a design of an invaluable 'manual' system of perforated sheets given to them by the Poles along with the AVA machine. This helped to break Luftwaffe and German Army keys in what was known as 'real time', allowing counteraction to be taken.

German Navy analysts worked in Hut 8 with the many times chess champion, C.H. Alexander, mostly in charge. Deciphered messages from Hut 6 were sent to Hut 3 for translation, appreciation and dissemination. German naval signal decrypts were worked on in Hut 4. Other teams studied methods of recording and analysis of the pattern of German signal traffic, tell-tale call signs, mistakes and careless repetitions filed in shoe boxes. Such sensitive work was rigorously compartmentalised so that people knew little or nothing about what went on in neighbouring huts.

Soon four Bombes in a hut surrounded by thick steel reinforced concrete were running keys through intercepts from fifty-nine enemy radio networks, all of them changing every 24 hours, sometimes every 12 hours. Later in the war the day's codes were often broken as early as 3 a.m. – a record time was 14 minutes.

By the end of the war more than 200 Bombes had been built at different locations, operated by 2,000 members of the Women's Royal Naval Service (Wrens) day and night. Later Bombes were named after towns and countries. In 1942 Americans joined the Bletchley staff, and later the US Navy developed Bombes that were faster than those at Bletchley.

With the millions of combinations of the Enigma machine, Bletchley's work had hit-or-miss aspects that required a determined try, try and try again attitude, and immense patience through countless disappointments. The Bombes depended on cribs and these were helped by German operators making errors in procedure. To find a crib Bletchley had to know who was sending signals to whom, and the likely gist of the message. This required current knowledge of the radio traffic pattern, together with decodes of recent messages.

It was not until the disastrous Norwegian campaign

in April 1940 that the teams at Bletchley began to read the first German Army and Air Force messages, at that time mainly about routine matters like postings. Within Germany's borders most signals went via landlines, but when operations took German forces abroad they relied on radio communications to coordinate air and ground units during their rapid advances. German signals operating procedures changed suddenly on 1 May 1940, defeating a system Bletchley had been using to read enemy army and air messages and placing immediate reliance on success with the Bombes. On 10 May the Germans began their new blitzkrieg offensive across western Europe.

Despite that, as Gen Heinz Guderian's panzer columns drove through the old Flanders battlefields in two days and onwards deep into France, Guderian's orders sent by radio from an Enigma machine travelling with him were intercepted. Enough German Army messages were decoded to make it clear that French resistance was collapsing, but this difficult task took so long that by the time the information reached field headquarters the British commander there had already reached the same conclusion and ordered the evacuation of the British Expeditionary Force from Dunkirk and the muster of an armada of little ships to carry most of them back across the Channel.

Cdr Denniston became ill during this critical time and Edward Travis, who had combined leading the naval section with being Denniston's deputy, succeeded him in February 1942 and ran Bletchley for the rest of the war.

During the Battle of Britain in the autumn of 1940 the quality of the intercepts greatly improved and deciphering delays were cut to a few hours. The Luftwaffe chief, Marshal Herman Goering, who could easily have used landlines for communications with his squadrons, fortunately had confidence in the Enigma code and issued his daily orders to his squadrons by radio. These signals revealed that his strategy was aimed at drawing all British fighter squadrons into mass air battles so that superior German numbers could destroy them quickly.

Reading the enemy commander's own words on his strategy and tactics enabled AM Hugh Dowding, the Fighter Command chief, to take a daily heavy toll of the Luftwaffe squadrons while carefully shepherding his own. He was criticised by other RAF fighter chiefs who favoured what was called Big Wing interceptions, but Dowding was unable to reveal even to senior officers that his strategy was based on Ultra.

After weeks of battle Goering's losses mounted and he switched from daylight attacks on RAF airfields to night attacks on London and other cities – a critical mistake. By that time the RAF had only a handful of fighter aircraft in reserve. Had the Luftwaffe succeeded in completely wiping out or grounding our fighter squadrons the waters around southern England would have been untenable to our shipping, and Operation Sealion, Hitler's invasion plan for October, would have gone ahead against an army that had abandoned most of its tanks and guns in its flight from the continent.

By autumn the mansion at Bletchley Park was surrounded by clusters of huts to provide work space for the growing staff. By this time much Enigma intelligence was being deciphered and disseminated in time to influence operations. As fast as they were deciphered they were sent to Hut 3 where the signals were rewritten in a way that presented the information accurately but in a manner that could not relate it to an

Enigma signal. These sanitised versions were sent to Sir Stewart Menzies, who as head of the Secret Intelligence Service was in overall command of Bletchley Park. He took the most important ones personally to Winston Churchill and the military chiefs. They were passed through Special Liaison Units to military commanders overseas. All material gathered from high grade signals intelligence went under the code name Ultra with guidelines aimed at ensuring that operations to counter German moves avoided any risk of revealing that Allied intelligence had been obtained by breaking Enigma transmissions. The security of Ultra had the highest priority of all. But while Ultra intelligence about the formation of a German Afrika Korps, the movement of Stuka dive-bombing squadrons to Sicily, and a German move into the Balkans and Greece to cover the flank of a planned invasion of the Soviet Union was flowing to Army and Air Force operations rooms, the German Navy's codes remained secure for another year.

This was proving costly, with the losses of ships and crews mounting as the U-boats sought to cut supplies and starve Britain into surrender. The German Navy chiefs, determined to avoid the breaking of their codes, as had happened in 1914, were much more security-minded than the other services, and their signals personnel were better trained in avoiding repetitions of code groups that could provide clues to code-breaking cryptanalysts. The German Navy had its own version of Enigma ciphers known as 'Schlussel M' (Key M), which involved thirteen different ciphers. The most important of these for the Bletchley Park naval code breakers was the Heimische Gewasser (Home waters) network, abridged to Heimisch and later renamed Hydra, the cipher used by U-boats in the North Atlantic and known at Bletchley as Dolphin.

Bletchley's maximum effort went into attempts to break the almost infinite number of naval Enigma settings, and with the Germans introducing frequent amendments this posed an unending challenge. The Admiralty also kept signals intelligence in its own hands, and from the moment war began the Navy was intent on capturing a German naval vessel in the hope of repeating their good fortune in the First World War. In November 1914 valuable German ciphers were recovered from beneath the wreck of the enemy light cruiser *Magdeburg* which ran aground in fog off the Russian Baltic island of Odensholm. The Czarist Navy passed the documents on to the Admiralty, enabling Room 40 to break German naval signals, an advantage, as stated earlier, that some tradition-bound admirals tended to ignore.

The first similar break in the Second World War came in February 1940, when the *U-33* was sunk by the minesweeper HMS *Gleaner* while on a minelaying mission in the Clyde estuary. Before abandoning ship the captain took the three rotors from the Enigma machine and five others from a box, handed some of them to two crew members with instructions to dump them into the sea as they jumped overboard. Later three rotors were recovered from the pockets of a rescued seaman who later confessed to his captain that in the stress of abandoning ship he had forgotten about them. These rotors helped the cryptanalysts in Hut 8, but a solution of the naval Enigma still eluded them.

A real break came in May 1940, after British destroyers stopped a trawler off Norway on 26 April that was flying Dutch colours, suspecting that it was a disguised German Navy vessel. As a whaler from HMS *Griffin* approached with a boarding party a man was seen throwing two canvas bags overboard. One sank and the other floated. Master Gunner F.H.W.T. Foord jumped from the whaler with a heaving line and almost drowned before he and the bag he clung to were hauled aboard the whaler. The bag was found to contain cipher forms, not cipher settings as wrongly stated in the British official history. Other cipher papers were found strewn about the armed trawler, *Schiff 26*, after she was boarded. The captured cipher forms, containing matching plain and cipher text, helped the cryptanalysts at Bletchley Park to make the first decrypts of the German naval Enigma. At last Bletchley was reading some naval Enigma messages retrospectively, but they were still little nearer the break needed. These decrypts contained little of intelligence value and took a month to decrypt, but they were a critically important part of the process which eventually led to Bletchley Park breaking the Heimisch ciphers.

Almost a year passed, during which the naval section had little to work on save radio traffic analysis and the volume and flow of German naval signals. A picture of organisation of German naval communications was compiled from direction finding, frequencies and addresses. Analysts looked for deviations from normal traffic patterns reflecting unusual activity.

At this period most cribs came from what Bletchley termed 'kisses', identical messages transmitted in two cryptosystems, one of which Bletchley could read. Hut 4, which handled non-Enigma naval messages, was reading the German Navy's Dockyard Cipher, and some messages sent in Dockyard Cipher were also sent to U-boats on the Enigma system. But in the absence of up-to-date intelligence from intercepted signals the Submarine Tracking Room at the Admiralty mainly relied on the Direction Finding Section, whose information came from operating stations around Britain, and at Gibraltar and Iceland.

Ten months passed before the next naval Enigma material was sent to Bletchley Park. In February 1941 a set of spare rotors, cipher documents and charts were captured during a commando raid on the Lofoten Islands. They were found by a boarding party in a burning trawler named *Krebs*, but the Enigma machine had already been thrown overboard. The rotors were identical to those already in Bletchley's hands, but one document gave the February Enigma keys. Room 8 made good use of this and for a week from 12 March many deciphered messages were sent by teleprinter to the Operational Intelligence Centre before they tailed off. Despite that, useful information still came. Cryptanalysts read part of the back traffic for February within five weeks, and subsequently they broke into messages sent in April and then into much of the May traffic.

Since the summer of 1940, needing weather information for their bombing blitz and their planned invasion, the Germans had been sending weather reporting ships into the Atlantic. The Navy sank two of them before Harry Hinsley, recruited to Bletchley while still an undergraduate, suggested that as weather-ships stayed at sea for months they would have to carry Enigma keys for the whole time they were likely to be at sea. He put the idea of capturing one to Capt J.R.S. Haines, assistant director of the Admiralty's Operational Intelligence Centre, and in May 1941 a strong Royal Navy task force raided the German weather reporting ship *Muenchen*. It was led by Vice Adm Lancelot Holland in the cruiser HMS *Edinburgh*, accompanied by the destroyers *Somali*, *Eskimo*, *Bedouin* and *Nestor*.

Just inside the Arctic Circle at 1707 hr on 7 May, the *Muenchen* was sighted by the *Somali*, which fired warning shots. The German crew began to abandon ship and the *Somali* went alongside and boarded her. They were quickly joined by a prize crew from the *Edinburgh*, accompanied by Capt Haines in civilian clothes. The captain of the *Muenchen* had thrown the Enigma coding machine overboard as the *Somali* approached, but Haines found what he was looking for on his cabin desk – coding tables for May and June. HMS *Nestor* raced back to Scapa Flow with Capt Haines, who carried the captured material to London. The documents enabled Bletchley to read German signals with minimum delay, until they were routinely changed six weeks later. (On 12 May Vice Adm Holland transferred to HMS *Hood*, and twelve days later he and most of the battleship's crew were killed when the *Hood* was sunk in minutes by salvoes from the German battleship *Bismarck*'s more powerful guns.) The Germans were misled into believing that the Enigma was still secure by a carefully worded official Admiralty communiqué which told of the incident in these words: 'One of our patrols operating in northern waters encountered the Muenchen, a German armed trawler. Fire was opened and the crew of the Muenchen then abandoned and scuttled their ship. They were subsequently rescued and made prisoner.'

On 9 May, just two days after the capture of the weather-ship documents, material of the highest grade was captured. The destroyers *Bulldog*, *Broadway* and *Aubretia* were escorting Convoy OB318 south of Iceland when the *U-110*, which had already sunk two ships in the convoy, was picked up by Asdic, the underwater direction-finding radar. Depth-charge attacks wrecked the U-boat's hydroplane and rudder, and with all power and lighting lost and water surging in, Kapitanleutnant Fritz-Julius Lemp ordered all tanks to be blown and the U-boat lurched to the surface. The flotilla commander, Capt A.J. Baker Cresswell of *Bulldog*, ordered his gun crews to open fire and set course to ram, but just in time he remembered a staff college lecture about the capture of valuable German ciphers from the light cruiser *Magdeburg* in 1914, and to the surprise of all his fellow escort commanders he ordered all offensive action to cease. But the *Broadway* also seemed to be intent on ramming the U-boat, despite the *Bulldog*'s captain shouting 'Stand clear' through his megaphone, while a signal lamp flashed the same order. In fact the *Broadway* was intent on dropping two depth charges beneath the U-boat to prevent her crash-diving, and unwittingly was on a collision course because firing her 4-in guns had cracked the bridge windscreen so badly it was almost opaque. She passed so close that the U-boat's hydroplane cut her port forward fuel tank, spilling oil into the sea.

Kapitanleutnant Lemp had seen the destroyer bearing down on him from the conning tower, and shouted to his crew to abandon ship. The guns were silent while the crew came out of the conning tower and jumped into the sea, to be picked up by boats from the *Broadway* and the corvette *Aubretia*. The U-boat's captain, the man who had sunk the *Athenia* on the day war began, was not among them. Those rescued were taken aboard the two ships and quickly hustled below so that they could not see a boat from the *Bulldog* putting a boarding party on their abandoned U-boat.

A twenty-year-old sub-lieutenant, David Balme, in charge of the boarding party, climbed down the ladder inside the conning tower and organised the lifting of a machine that looked like a typewriter, guessing it was some kind of coding machine. It was unbolted and passed out to the whaler, along with equipment and documents that later filled two packing cases.

The U-boat was taken in tow, but on the way to Scapa Flow via Iceland next day she began to sink, and the tow line was reluctantly cut. This was to be of great relief to the Admiralty when they realised that the Enigma material seized without the enemy's knowledge was infinitely more valuable than a captured U-boat. Capt Baker Cresswell had the equivalent of the 1914 *Magdeburg* prize.

On the *Bulldog*'s return to Scapa Flow she was met by Lt Allon Bacon and a colleague assigned by Bletchley Park, who had brought a single briefcase to collect anything of special value. They were quickly in raptures over the appropriated material. They photographed the most important items in case of accident while transporting the treasure, in specially made containers, to Bletchley Park.

Hut 8 began work on it on 13 May. This material, combined with that from the weather-ship *Muenchen*, allowed U-boat messages to be read eleven days after interception. But when the captured Enigma keys for June came into force the Operation Intelligence Centre was at last able to read U-boat traffic in 'real time', almost as fast as the U-boat commanders and Doenitz himself. A German message intercepted at 18 minutes past midnight on 1 June was deciphered in

Hut 8, translated in Hut 4 and sent to the Operational Intelligence Centre by 4.58 a.m.

This was the most important intelligence breakthrough of the war to date. When Capt Baker Cresswell went to Buckingham Palace to receive the Distinguished Service Order, King George VI told him that his feat was one of the most significant events of the war at sea, and but for the necessity of security a higher award would have been made. Sub Lt Balme received the Distinguished Service Cross. (All records of this incident, like others, were expunged in Britain even in the official war history *The War at Sea*, edited by Capt S.W. Roskill, published in 1954.)

These captured materials were a godsend to Turing and his colleagues at Bletchley, but they came too late to influence the early stages of the hunt for the German battleship *Bismarck*, which had disappeared into the wide Atlantic after sinking the British battleship *Hood* on 24 May. But Ultra played a key role when the enemy battleship seemed likely to escape. Thinking he was still being shadowed by a British warship Adm Lutyens broke radio silence and sent a long signal about the damage his ship had incurred in the action, and asked his headquarters for further orders. However, this signal was not decrypted for three days, by which time the *Bismarck* had been sunk. The *Bismarck*'s position was obtained by direction finding, and it was a Luftwaffe signal that helped reveal that the *Bismarck*'s destination was Brest.

Although the *Bismarck* signals had taken at least three days to break, by June the time taken to decipher messages averaged less than six hours. Hydra, used for German ships in the North Sea and Baltic, for minesweepers and patrol craft off the French and

Norwegian coasts, and at that time for all U-boats, was at long last penetrated. Another early success came in June when Ultra reported that the pocket battleship *Lutzow*, formerly named *Deutschland*, was leaving the Baltic for the North Sea, giving her position, course and speed. She was intercepted by torpedo bombers, and so badly damaged she was out of action for many months.

RAF minelaying operations around German-controlled ports caused much signal traffic by German shipping involved in minesweeping, and these operations, called 'gardening' were extended in close cooperation with the code-breakers. This provided a series of successful cribs, and with the experience of working with the known settings captured by the *Bulldog*, gave Bletchley Park new insight. They were to go on reading Hydra messages, except for a few days, for the rest of the war. At last they were able to supply the Submarine Tracking Room at the Admiralty's Operational Intelligence Centre with a wealth of detailed information.

When the captured keys expired Harry Hinsley urged another operation to 'pinch' current Enigma material from another weather-ship, the *Lauenburg*, which had sailed from the northern Norwegian port of Trondheim in the last week of May to operate in an area 300 miles north of the Arctic Circle. The task force, a cruiser and three destroyers, set out and a lookout on the destroyer *Tartar* spotted her just before dusk on 28 June. But the strength of nearby radio signals picked up by the *Lauenburg*'s radio operator alerted the German crew to an enemy approach, and as shells fell around their ship the captain and most of his crew lowered two lifeboats. Two men left on board threw the Enigma machine overboard and began stuffing documents into the coal-burning furnace.

By the time the *Lauenburg* was boarded by the Allies there appeared to be nothing left but a litter of paper, thought to be rubbish. But to the men's surprise Lt Allon Bacon, the intelligence officer assigned by Bletchley Park to accompany the force in the destroyer *Jupiter*, joined them and ordered every document to be collected. They filled thirteen mail sacks, and among much dross Bacon found what he was looking for – the Enigma keys for July – as well as sheets for the plugboard, covering the whole of that month, and a sheet of internal settings. They reached Bletchley on 2 July, and from that date Bletchley was able to transcribe Enigma messages within three hours for the rest of that month.

Then came another long period when the signals traffic of operational U-boats became secure again. On 1 February 1942, U-boats were detached from Hydra and linked directly with Adm Doenitz by a new model Enigma called the M4 with a cipher called Triton, introduced the previous October. The naval cryptanalysts were stumped by Triton M4, the four-rotor Enigma, which they code-named Shark, and intelligence about U-boats at sea was reduced to slim pickings from Hydra, mainly relying on direction-finding and the Submarine Tracking Room's deep knowledge of patterns of U-boat behaviour.

There was deep despair among the chiefs at Bletchley Park when the four-rotor Enigma was introduced. Most of them believed that the task of breaking it was impossible. Alan Turing disagreed and said he would solve it. About the same time, the Germans also introduced a new Meteorological Code, invalidating the 1941 Met Code captured by HMS *Bulldog* ten months before. This had provided invaluable entry into solving Enigma traffic because U-boats at sea regularly transmitted weather reports, and for brevity these messages were encrypted in the three-letter group weather code before being reciphered in the current Enigma key. This change halted comparison of the Met Code with Enigma. While the Navy's intelligence about U-boat operations was virtually blacked out, the German equivalent to Bletchley Park, Beobachtungdienst (observation service), had broken the Royal Navy's code No. 3, introduced in June 1941 as the common encryption system between British, Canadian and United States warships covering the Atlantic convoy routes. This gave Doenitz 'real time' intelligence, enabling his chiefs to plot the routes of convoys as much as 12 hours in advance of their sailing. This huge gap in Allied intelligence and German reading of our convoy preparations, details of shipping and escorts, speed and routes came at the very time Adm Doenitz launched a new U-boat offensive in a maximum effort to starve Britain into seeking an armistice. He had begun 1942 with 249 U-boats in service and their sinkings of Allied vessels had totalled 700,000 tons in June and 730,000 in November. By January 1943, he had 400 U-boats under his command. Most of them were equipped for improved offensive quality, manned by experienced crews, and fitted with a new electronic device that warned of the approach of radar-equipped aircraft, allowing them time to dive to safety. Adm Doenitz was confident that the war-decisive battle which he believed would bring German victory was within his grasp.

Chapter Three

The Atlantic Battle – Dominating Campaign of the Second World War

The first six months of the Second World War became known as the 'phoney war'. All was quiet on the deeply fortified French Maginot Line; the British Expeditionary Force in France was not in action; there were none of the feared mass air raids and gas attacks on London and other cities; and the RAF's main task seemed to be dropping propaganda leaflets over Germany. But there was nothing phoney about the war at sea. It was waged in earnest from the first day.

At 11 a.m. on Sunday 3 September 1939 the Prime Minister, Neville Chamberlain, architect of the appeasement policy that had made Britain unprepared for war, broadcast to the nation to say what a bitter blow it was to him that Britain was again at war with Germany. The German dictator Adolf Hitler had ignored an ultimatum to withdraw German troops, who had invaded Poland three days before. Ominously France delayed declaring war until 5 p.m.

At 9 o'clock that same evening the 13,581-ton liner *Athenia*, en route to Montreal with 1,103 passengers and 305 crew, was torpedoed and sunk off Rockall with the loss of 118 lives, including 28 Americans and children being evacuated to safety from expected air raids. This tragic start to the war at sea was reminiscent of the sinking of the liner *Lusitania* in 1915 with the loss of 1,198 people, including 128 Americans, which began unrestricted U-boat warfare that brought America into the war in 1917.

(The submarine was originally conceived as a terrorist weapon. It was the brainchild of John Philip Holland, a member of the Irish Fenian Brotherhood, who wanted to cause a terrorist sensation by blowing up a British battleship. He emigrated to America where he developed the first submarine for the United States Navy, and designed the Royal Navy's first five submarines. It was propelled on the surface by an oil-fuel engine, which recharged batteries of an electric motor used when the vessel was submerged, electric power not needing an oxygen supply. It submerged by filling ballast tanks with sea water and surfaced by expelling the water by compressed air.)

On the day war was declared Winston Churchill became First Lord of the Admiralty, a post from which he had been forced to resign after the failure of the Dardanelles campaign in the First World War, and the German propaganda chief, Dr Josef Goebbels, claimed that Churchill had ordered British destroyers to torpedo the ship for propaganda purposes. Goebbels later admitted that an overenthusiastic U-boat commander had mistaken the liner for a troopship. Churchill regarded this as meaning unrestricted U-boat warfare and immediately ordered merchant ships to sail in convoys with naval escorts, a practice introduced in the First World War only after years of heavy shipping losses.

After Hitler came to power in 1933 the naval commander-in-chief, Adm Erich Raeder, had been told to be ready for war with Britain by 1944, and when Britain declared war over Poland, Chamberlain having merely wrung his hands over Hitler's takeover of Czechoslovakia, the German Navy chiefs felt ill-equipped to take on the world's leading naval power. However, in the last weeks of peace Adm Raeder decided to take the initiative at sea, and deployed two new battleships as well as eighteen U-boats in the Atlantic in readiness to sink British and Allied merchant ships, the start of the determined effort to starve Britain into submission. One of the battleships, the *Admiral Graf Spee*, sank nine merchant ships in the South Atlantic before she met three British cruisers in the Battle of the River Plate in December, retreating damaged into the Uruguayan port of Montevideo; she was scuttled a few days later. The other battleship, the *Deutschland*, sank only two ships before returning to port with engine trouble. She was in such disfavour with Hitler that he ordered a change of name to *Lutzow*.

The British public were greatly cheered by this first victory in the South Atlantic. Until then, while the Navy was clearly seen by the British public as the only ones fighting in earnest, there had been little but news of U-boat triumphs: just two weeks after war began a U-boat sank the aircraft carrier *Courageous*; in October another U-boat penetrated the defences of the main fleet base at Scapa Flow and sank the battleship *Royal Oak*; and in November the armed merchant cruiser *Rawalpindi* was sunk after signalling that she had spotted the *Deutschland* (in fact it was the *Scharnhorst*).

More naval cheer came two months after the sinking of the *Graf Spee* when the destroyer HMS *Cossack* boarded the *Graf Spee*'s supply ship, the *Altmark*, in a Norwegian fjord and rescued 299 members of crews of the ships the battleship had sunk. AB James Harper's shout to the prisoners held below decks – 'The Navy's Here' – made heartening headlines.*

This exploit also gave an indication of the large number of merchant ships being sunk. There were, of course, no public announcements about losses in the unrelenting struggle against the U-boat threat to Britain's ocean lifelines. The Atlantic battle was the longest and most important struggle of the Second World War as it had been in the First World War. (In April 1917, the worst month of both world wars, U-boats sank 881,000 tons of merchant shipping, reducing Britain's essential supplies to three weeks. Altogether 4,837 ships, totalling 11,135,000 tons were lost. U-boat losses numbered 178 and 176 surrendered in November 1918.)

Despite the crippling losses of 1914–18, in 1939 the British merchant shipping fleet was the largest in the world, comprising nearly one-third of all shipping, equalling the combined total of the three nearest shipping rivals, the United States, Japan and Norway. When Norway was occupied most of its merchant ships were at sea, and all sailed to British ports. So, subsequently, did most Danish, Dutch and Belgian ships. Later, a large Greek fleet joined the Allied shipping fleet. Altogether this gave Britain the use of an extra 700 ships, and with 480,000 tons of shipping hired from the

---

* The author's uncle was awared the DSM for his part in the rescue.

neutral Swedes, provided 3 million tons of shipping capacity – a 25 per cent increase.

In 1937, with another war looming, the Admiralty had set up the Shipping Defence Advisory Committee, and liaison officers trained merchant seamen in ship defence. Hundreds of ships had their decks stiffened to mount anti-aircraft guns, and thousands of seamen had been instructed in gunnery.

At the end of the First World War the powerful German High Seas Fleet, a total of seventy-four ships, sailed to Scapa Flow to surrender and before the ships could be shared between the victorious nations, they were scuttled by their own crews. The terms of the dictated Versailles Peace Treaty allowed its replacement by only a token force, and imposed a total ban on the construction of U-boats. In 1922 German U-boat designers formed a company in Holland to continue their work, designing and advising on submarines for Japan, Sweden, Argentina, Spain and Turkey. Former U-boat commander, Wilhelm Canaris, later chief of Hitler's military intelligence service, was involved. U-boat components were shipped from the factory in Holland to the German Baltic port of Kiel, where they were assembled in concealed sheds.

Karl Doenitz, who won the Iron Cross in the First World War, took over command of the three U-boats of the first flotilla in September 1935, and was made Führer der U-boote (Chief of Submarines), a year later. He had commanded a U-boat in the Mediterranean, and been captured by the British after scuttling his damaged craft in October 1918. He feigned insanity and spent some time in a Manchester mental hospital before obtaining early release in July 1919 when he returned to the Kriegsmarine to command a torpedo boat.

When war was renewed Doenitz was determined to win the Atlantic struggle, driven by the knowledge of how close U-boats had brought Britain to asking for an armistice in 1917, and embittered at having the tables turned, with the British naval blockade forcing a starving Germany instead to ask for an armistice in 1918. In this second round Doenitz's vengeful intention was to succeed in starving Britain into defeat. But in 1938 Hitler had drawn up what was called the Z plan for a fleet of super-battleships able to drive the British Navy from the seas. The plan also promised Doenitz the 300 U-boats he said he needed before war with Britain was resumed. But war came earlier than Hitler expected, and only three pocket battleships of just under 12,000 tons were completed. They had been specifically designed for commerce raiding and not for taking on British battleships, but they compared favourably in speed, armament and armour with the Royal Navy's ageing battleships.

Meanwhile, the British Navy was much reduced by economic necessity as well as calls for disarmament. As early as 1922, under controversial Washington Naval Treaties, 12 of the Navy's 27 battleships were scrapped, and cuts were made in all other branches. When war began the Royal Navy had 12 battleships, 3 battle-cruisers, 62 cruisers, 7 aircraft carriers, and 2 seaplane carriers. The German Navy's surface fleet comprised the battlecruisers *Scharnhorst* and *Gneisenau*, 3 pocket battleships, 6 cruisers, 17 destroyers and other support craft. The super-battleships *Bismarck* and *Tirpitz*, the aircraft carrier *Graf Zeppelin* and 4 heavy cruisers were still under construction. While the German surface fleet stayed mainly in harbour, the Royal Navy had to deploy its own heavy ships for most of the war to cover the

constant threat of attack and react to the few actual
sallies against merchant ships from this comparatively
small number of major ships. From the beginning to
the end the U-boat was the German Navy's prime
weapon and the destroyer its main adversary. When
the Atlantic struggle began the Royal Navy had only
165 destroyers, many dating from the First World
War. There were also 35 sloops and 20 trawlers fitted
with Asdic, a new submarine detection device to
combat the U-boats. In the last years of peace orders
had been placed to fill the need for convoy escorts
with corvettes and other types of cheap, quickly built
vessels. In December 1940 after Churchill had written
to President Franklin Roosevelt of Britain's mortal
danger from the steady and increasing diminution
of shipping tonnage, the United States gave Britain
fifty old destroyers in exchange for naval bases in the
British West Indies, Bermuda and Newfoundland.

Because war came earlier than anticipated Doenitz
had only 57 U-boats at his disposal instead of the
300 he considered necessary to impose a tight blockade
on Britain. Of these 32 were short-range boats that
could voyage no further than the North Sea or around
British ports where shipping lines converged. These small
250-ton U-boats achieved notable success until British
defensive measures made their coastal operations too
costly. After Hitler's invasion of the Soviet Union in June
1941, these smaller U-boats were based in northern
Norway and made murderous attacks on convoys
carrying Allied war supplies – which were vital to keep
the Red Army fighting – to the northern Russian port of
Murmansk. Some of them were also sent to the eastern
Mediterranean in an effort to protect Rommel's supply
ships.

The other U-boats, capable of manoeuvres across Britain's western approaches, the focal point of operations aimed at the blockade of Britain, were mainly 626 tons with a range of over 6,000 miles, carrying eleven torpedoes and a crew of forty-four.

After war began the Germany Navy gave U-boat production the highest priority and ordered a vast construction programme for the larger U-boats. It became the standard Atlantic U-boat, and 705 were constructed at thirteen shipyards. Later came 1,000-ton U-boats armed with twenty-two torpedoes and tanker U-boats of 2,000 tons able to resupply fourteen U-boats with fuel, provisions, torpedoes and other supplies. (None of these were true submarines, but submersibles: they had to come up for air to run the diesels to recharge the batteries that propelled the underwater propulsion motors. Because the size of the batteries limited the range of these motors, U-boats cruised to their patrol stations at night on the surface using their diesel engines.)

For the Army and the RAF in Britain the 'phoney war' ended with a German invasion of Denmark and Norway in March 1940. The Navy escorted landings of British, French and Polish troops at several ports in mid-Norway and had to evacuate them soon afterwards because of the ferocity of German dive-bombing, the first of many hard-learned lessons that land-based air superiority was essential to naval and land operations.

Later, at the northerly port of Narvik, where Germany's super-destroyers had landed troops, the Navy fought two fierce destroyer actions with guns and torpedoes, and sank or crippled the ten enemy destroyers. This opened the way for the capture of the port and the landing of 25,000 Allied troops with cover from RAF Hurricane and biplane Gladiator fighter squadrons established on captured airfields. This first Allied success, in an otherwise disastrous campaign, was short-lived. In June, as the full weight of the German blitzkrieg tactics of panzer columns, supported by Stuka dive-bombing, set western Europe ablaze, the campaign in Norway had to be abandoned. Allied troops were evacuated from Narvik, and the Hurricane and Gladiator pilots who had fought off the Stukas made their first deck landings on the aircraft carrier *Glorious*. Most of them died when the *Glorious* ran into the German battlecruisers *Scharnhorst* and *Gneisenau* the following afternoon. The *Glorious* was sunk along with her two escorting destroyers, the *Ardent* and *Acasta*, though a torpedo from the *Acasta* damaged the *Scharnhorst* badly enough to force her back to port. These were only part of the heavy toll the Navy paid off Norway, but far more serious damage was inflicted on German Navy ships.

Some British warships and merchant vessels survived U-boat attacks because of torpedo failures. The U-boat ace, Gunther Prien, complained to Doenitz that he would have sunk the battleship *Warspite*, but for having what he called a 'wooden gun', and there were grievances from other U-boat commanders. The firing pistol was found to be the cause, and until the Germans developed a fully reliable pistol in 1942 the Germans used a copy of a British contact pistol they had found aboard a British minelaying submarine, HMS *Seal*, after it had surrendered to a German seaplane in the Skagerrak in May.

The British Navy suffered more heavy losses in the rescue of the British Expeditionary Force from the beaches of Dunkirk. The destroyer was the largest warship the Admiralty could risk sending inshore and, of the 39 destroyers engaged, 6 were sunk and

19 damaged by bombing. This was soon followed by the unimaginable disaster of the fall of France and the loss of an Allied navy with 5 battleships, 1 aircraft carrier, 15 cruisers, 75 destroyers and 59 submarines. Churchill, who had just taken over the premiership from Chamberlain, ordered desperate action to prevent these warships falling into German hands. The French Adm Darlan refused to send them to the French colonial island of Martinique in the West Indies and Adm Sir James Somerville, commanding the British Mediterranean Fleet, reluctantly carried out orders to sink capital ships of its recent ally at Oran, with heavy loss of life. This ruthlessness was also intended to signal that Britain was determined to carry on the fight until the bitter end, with no thought of seeking an armistice. The French Navy had been expected to play a major role in dealing with the Italian Navy, and Italy's entry into the war a few days before the French collapse stretched the Royal Navy even further. The Italian fleet comprised 6 battleships, 19 cruisers, 61 destroyers and 105 submarines. During the daunting year of 1940 when the RAF's near-run victory in the Battle of Britain made Hitler put off invading that autumn, the German occupation of the whole 3,000-mile coastline of western Europe, from the Arctic to the Spanish frontier, posed a new, potentially deadly longer-term threat.

It put the U-boat fleet on the doorstep of Britain's key western approaches, greatly increasing the vulnerability of shipping along Britain's supply lifelines, and marked the opening stage in the Battle of the Atlantic, the war's longest and most vital campaign. It meant the U-boats could operate as far west as 25 degrees, well into the gap between the end of escorts for convoys sailing from Halifax and their being under escort again on entering the western approaches.

Britain's foresight during the German invasion of Denmark and Norway, in countering likely German moves against the Danish Faroe Islands and the mid-North Atlantic island of Iceland, was to prove invaluable. But the neutral Irish Free State, independent since 1921, refused Britain's request to move back into two former naval bases in exchange for a promise to negotiate unity with the six loyalist counties of Northern Ireland after the war. Use of those bases would have moved protection of shipping 200 miles westwards, undoubtedly saving British ships and lives. Instead, the bays of Ireland sometimes provided shelter for U-boats.

Enough of the larger U-boats were coming into service for Adm Doenitz to make immediate use of the proximity of U-boat bases on the French coast to the Atlantic convoy routes.As early as 5 July the *U-30* (commanded by Fritz Lemp) was re-based at Lorient on the shores of the Bay of Biscay. Soon afterwards eight flotillas were operating from Brest, Lorient, La Pallice and Saint-Nazaire. They also used harbours in Fascist, but non-belligerent, Spain and her Atlantic Canary Islands for refuelling. The tactics were for long-range Focke-Wulfe Condor reconnaissance aircraft, based in Norway and France, to find a convoy, radio its course, speed and number of escorts to U-boat headquarters at Lorient, which would then order as many as ten U-boats in the area to form a patrol line ahead of the convoy moving at the speed of the slowest ship.

That first month of operations from Biscay ports thirty-eight ships (totalling 382,000 tons) were sunk, still fewer than a quarter of the number sunk in the worst months of 1917, but the outlook was stark. In August Hitler lifted all restrictions on U-boat targets, and that month's Allied shipping losses rose to 394,000 tons, and to 442,000 in September. In October 34 ships sailed for Britain at 7 knots in the slow Convoy SC7 and 17 were sunk and 2 more damaged in Adm Doenitz's first application of Rudeltaktik – U-boats hunting in wolf-packs. Convoy HX79 was attacked at the same time by another wolf-pack, but lost only a quarter of its ships because of heavier escorts. This concentration of U-boats swamped the small numbers of warships available to escort every convoy.

The pocket battleships were a constant threat. In November 1940 the new pocket battleship *Scheer* sank the British merchant cruiser *Jervis Bay* when her captain, posthumously awarded the Victoria Cross, ordered the convoy he was escorting to scatter while he engaged the far more powerful guns of the enemy. The *Scheer* evaded pursuit and operated in the South Atlantic and the Indian Ocean before making it safely back to Kiel in April 1941, having sunk fourteen merchant ships as well as the *Jervis Bay*, and captured two prizes. More serious than the loss of the 100,000 tons of shipping she sank was the prolonged disruption of convoys and naval dispositions she caused. Atlantic shipping and their crews were also falling prey to long-range Condor bombers, and to meet this Hurricane fighters were catapulted from merchant ships' decks. After engaging a Condor the Hurricane pilot's survival depended on ditching in the ocean beside the ship and being picked up. Only one Condor was shot down by a Hurricane, but this measure succeeded in preventing most Condors from approaching too close to convoys.

U-boats operating in the Atlantic increased by a third from January to April 1941. In two months 142 ships, totalling 815,000 tons, were sunk with vital cargoes of food and war materials. It was at this crucially low mark in the Battle of the Atlantic that Churchill made the moving broadcast referred to on page 10. Adm Doenitz's own son-in-law, Cdr Gunter Hesser, in the *U-107* sank fourteen ships, totalling 86,700 tons, towards the end of the following May and early June – a record bag for a single patrol.

In May Adm Raeder sent the battleship *Bismarck* (41,700 tons) and the heavy cruiser *Prinz Eugen* into the North Atlantic with the expectation that they would strike much heavier blows against convoys carrying supplies to Britain. The plan was for *Bismarck* to take on British warships while the *Prinz Eugen* went after convoys. During a chase by British battleships the *Bismarck*'s 15-in guns hit the ancient HMS *Hood*'s ammunition stores and she blew up. Of her crew of 1,419 only 3 were picked up by rescuers. *Bismarck* then disappeared, but thanks to Ultra reporting her signals traffic, she was cornered and sunk after massive attacks by British ships and planes.

As in the first Atlantic campaign in 1914–18 the Germans fitted merchant ships with 5.9-in guns and torpedoes to prey on ships sailing without escort in remote parts of the world. Six of them left German ports in the spring of 1940 after meticulous arrangements were made for them to be refuelled like U-boats, mainly at sea. The disguised raiders and U-boats were informed of the remote ocean locations of their 'milch cows' before sailing because the supply ships maintained strict radio silence. That meant Ultra was unable to trace them. But soon after the *Bismarck* hunt, all six milch cows were sunk after being spotted by ships or aircraft.

In November 1941, the most successful of the disguised raiders, the *Atlantis*, on her way home after sinking twenty-two ships totalling over 150,000 tons – three times as much as the *Graf Spee* – since leaving Germany in March 1940, was ordered to resupply U-boats in the South Atlantic. This change of role had to be ordered by radio, and Ultra intelligence was able to pinpoint the area to which she was diverted. On 22 November the cruiser *Devonshire*'s seaplane spotted a suspicious merchant ship, and later the *Devonshire* sighted her while she was refuelling a U-boat. The U-boat crash-dived, and the *Atlantis* ended her disguise as a Dutch ship and uncovered her guns, but then ordered the crew to abandon ship. The *Devonshire* opened fire and the *Atlantis* went down. Because of the known presence of a U-boat the British sailed away without picking up survivors, but *U-126* returned and picked up 308 of her crew, towing lifeboats for three days to put them aboard the U-boat supply ship *Python*.

This involved another break in radio silence, and Ultra pinpointed the *Python*'s position. On 1 December the *Devonshire*'s sister ship, HMS *Dorsetshire*, caught her refuelling two U-boats. Again the U-boats escaped but the *Python* was sunk and her crew and survivors from the *Atlantis*, 414 in all, were again rescued by the on-scene U-boats. These were later joined by two other U-boats and four Italian submarines, when lifeboats were discarded, and the crammed submarines reached Saint-Nazaire during Christmas. Two other merchant raiders were sunk during this time, while three made it back to European ports. Providing surface vessels for the supply of U-boats was abandoned because of these British successes. Preparations had already begun to resupply U-boats at sea from a new type of U-boat, and the first came into service that December.

Two decisions by Hitler reduced Atlantic losses

at the end of 1941. First Hitler ordered a reluctant Doenitz to transfer twenty-three U-boats to the eastern Mediterranean to stem the losses the Royal Navy was inflicting on ships carrying supplies to the Afrika Korps. Then Hitler declared war on the United States on 9 December, shortly after the Japanese attack on Pearl Harbor. Doenitz sent long-range 1,000-ton U-boats to attack shipping off the eastern seaboard of America, and the U-boats enjoyed what their crews called a 'Happy Time'. The smaller 500-ton U-boats, refuelled by the first tanker U-boats known to the Allies as 'milch cows', were able to join in.

In their operations on the far side of the ocean the U-boat crews were favoured by two factors: American resort towns on the Atlantic observed no blackouts and offshore shipping was often silhouetted against them; and the American Navy's chief, Adm Ernest King, regarded the convoy system as a defensive measure inappropriate to the traditions of the US Navy.

King was so intent on avenging the Japanese for Pearl Harbor that his main focus was always on the Pacific war, and the British, Canadian and the exiled Allied navies bore the brunt of the key Atlantic battle. Between January and July 1942 460 ships (totalling 2.3 million tons), including tankers from Venezuela, were sunk off the American eastern seaboard. The convoy system was at last introduced in April with the help of twenty-five ships that the Royal Navy could not really spare, and losses fell. Later the Americans used small spotter airships called 'Blimps' with convoys, and they proved most effective.

Meanwhile, in February 1942, the German Navy pulled off a marvellous propaganda coup, an action that stunned the British people as much as the fall of the

British Navy's Singapore bastion to the Japanese was to dismay them a few days later. After lying idle and much bombed in the French port of Brest in February 1942, the *Scharnhorst*, *Gneisenau* and *Prinz Eugen* succeeded in making a dash back to Germany through the Channel. Only the *Prinz Eugen* arrived unscathed through torpedo attacks by planes and destroyers, but ten days later she was torpedoed by the British submarine *Trident* off Norway and although she made harbour was never in action again. The two battleships were damaged by mines dropped in front of them by British planes, and the *Gneisenau* was completely crippled in three nights of bombing by the RAF. The *Scharnhorst* was under repair for six months.

The Germans hailed their escape from Brest as a triumph, but Adm Raeder admitted 'It was a tactical success but a strategic defeat.' For Britain it meant the only big ship threat now came from Norwegian waters.

The worst convoy disaster of the war came the following July as a result of the *Tirpitz* moving its berth. Ultra intelligence reported this move as a threat to Convoy PQ17 on its way to Murmansk, and the Admiralty ordered the convoy to scatter. Massed Heinkel torpedo bombers and U-boats sank twenty-four of the thirty-five merchant ships. In fact Hitler had refused to risk the *Tirpitz*, and she merely changed berths. (Churchill told Stalin that the cost of sending him supplies by this shortest route was too high. Of 811 ships in 40 Russian convoys 92 were lost.)

Doenitz always believed that the North Atlantic was where the key victory could be won, and he obeyed Hitler's orders to disperse his U-boats to other theatres of war with great reluctance. He knew the decisive battle was the closure of the Atlantic supply routes to

Britain, and with more than his desired 300 U-boats at his disposal at last, and with much improved torpedoes, the most savage U-boat attacks of the war began in 1942. They became more brutal than ever after a tragic incident in September in which the *U-156*, one of the enlarged craft, sank the troopship *Laconia* carrying 2,600 men, including 1,800 Italian prisoners of war. When he paused to pick up survivors the U-boat captain, Cdr Werner Hartenstein, was shocked to find they were Italians, and sent out an international emergency radio message in English saying he would not attack rescuing ships. Hartenstein crammed his own craft with survivors, including some in British and Polish uniforms, and began towing four lifeboats towards the African coast. Other U-boats and Italian submarines also gathered and picked up more survivors. The following day, still far out at sea, an American Navy Liberator spotted them and despite the red cross Hartenstein had displayed on his conning tower, the pilot was ordered by radio to attack the U-boat. It made two desultory attacks, but did no damage. Doenitz immediately ordered the abandonment of the rescue; 800 Britons and Poles, but only 450 Italians, were eventually saved.

Shortly afterwards Doenitz issued a general order to all U-boats banning all attempts at rescuing people from ships they sank, or provisioning lifeboats. It stated, 'The rescue of survivors contradicts the elementary necessity of war for the destruction of enemy ships and crews.' This order might have brought Doenitz a death sentence when he was tried at Nuremburg with other Nazi leaders, but for evidence from Adm Chester Nimitz, the US Navy commander, who said that 'as a general rule US ships did not rescue survivors'. Instead, he was sentenced to ten years for waging aggressive war.

In Britain a court martial sentenced the commander and officers of the *U-852* to death by firing squad for machine-gunning survivors of the Greek merchant ship *Peleous* in March 1944.

The new U-boat offensive came at the time of the Anglo-American landings in French North Africa, and escorting the convoys there, some directly from America, severely reduced the number of escorts available to protect the vital North Atlantic convoys to Britain. During this period six Atlantic liners, including the *Queen Elizabeth* (84,000 tons) and the *Queen Mary* (81,000 tons) were relying on their speed of up to 30 knots to carry about 200,000 troops cross the Atlantic without escort. To avoid the risks of bombing they had been berthed in New York in the early part of the war, and had then been used as troopships carrying Australian divisions to the Middle East and later huge numbers of American troops to Australia – all without loss.

In November 1942 117 Allied merchant ships totalling 700,000 tons were sunk, and another 100,000 tons were lost through mines and bombing. Fierce gales restricted U-boat operations in December, reducing losses to 262,000 tons that month. The average monthly figure for losses during the whole year was 650,000 tons, twice the rate that new ships were coming into service. U-boat losses were only half the number of new ones being launched, and at the end of 1942 Doenitz had 212 U-boats compared with 91 at the beginning of the year.

The German naval staff had calculated that sinkings of 800,000 tons a month would stem the flow of food and essential war materials, and force a starving Britain to ask for an armistice. They seemed well on the way to achieving that disastrous rate of sinkings.

Chapter Four
The Victory Ship

On 27 March 1941, at Walker's shipyard in Newcastle upon Tyne – while battle raged in the Atlantic – the hull of a new warship was launched, a ship that was to play a key part in achieving the final victory that then seemed so remote.

There was no ceremony for such occasions in those dark wartime days. Only a handful of naval officers were among shipyard workers, their bosses and office staff watching the raw hull roll down the slipway into a rain-lashed River Tyne. Her construction had begun on Boxing Day 1939 and it had taken a further fourteen months to fit out the hull – moored to a jetty and untouched by enemy air raids – as a fighting ship. This work went on all summer and through the following bitter winter of 1941/2, the coldest in living memory and remembered later as the gloomiest period of the Second World War.

On 15 July 1942 the brand new warship was handed over to a mainly untried crew, most of them enlisted 'for hostilities only' and the white ensign was raised to commission her as the fleet destroyer HMS *Petard*, later to be adopted by the London Borough of Paddington during a national Warship Week. She was to have been named *Persistent*, but instead she was given a name described in dictionaries as 'a crude bombing device, liable to blow up in one's face before it could be planted on the enemy'. Not, one might think, entirely appropriate for a warship and not a name to give confidence to those of her crew who bothered to wonder about the name. In the First World War a destroyer named HMS *Petard* sank the German Navy's *V-29* torpedo boat – then the German equivalent of a destroyer, though smaller and less well armed – with a direct torpedo hit during the Battle of Jutland.

The Second World War's HMS *Petard* was to undergo a first commission that lived up to her name, packed with explosive action, some self-damaging. She became unique as the only Allied warship to sink submarines of all three enemy navies: German, Italian and Japanese. Despite her name, and against all odds, HMS *Petard* was to be one of only three out of eight P class destroyers to survive the war still serviceable.

They were classified fleet destroyers because they were fast and fully equipped with all armaments including torpedoes. Their fire-power consisted of 4 4-in guns, 1 four-barrel pom-pom also firing shells, and 4 oerlikon machine-guns, 8 torpedo tubes, and 100 depth charges. The ships were 388 ft long, 35 ft wide at the beam, weighed 1,540 tons and averaged a top speed of 32 knots, though the *Petard* could increase this to 34 knots. She carried a crew of 211, including 9 officers, almost double the complement for which she was originally designed.

The ratings (non-commissioned ranks) slept in hammocks slung between the forward deck spaces above the tables where they ate food brought from a tiny galley. Men kept their clothing and other belongings in small kitbag-sized compartments in padded benches, and did their own laundry (dhobied) in a bucket. The nine officers had luxurious individual cabins with wooden bunks and other furniture in comparatively spacious accommodation below the quarterdeck aft.

Her first captain was Lt Cdr S.H. Beattie, but while the *Petard* was still being built he was transferred to command the former American destroyer, *Campbelltown*, in which he won the Victoria Cross for ramming the gates on a dock built to hold the liner *Normandie* during a commando raid on the French port of Saint-Nazaire. The dock, the only one on the Atlantic seaboard big enough to hold the super-battleship *Tirpitz*, was knocked out until after the war.

Beattie was replaced by Lt Cdr Mark Thornton DSC, RN, who had previously commanded the fleet destroyer *Harvester* and had earned his Distinguished Service Cross sinking the *U-32* off Northern Ireland in October 1940. He was of medium height, stocky with grey close-cropped hair and the battered face of a boxer; a granite man. It was soon clear to the officers and senior crew members of the *Petard* that he was still stressed from his two years of rigorous Atlantic convoy duties in which the *Harvester* was also credited with sinking a second U-boat. (Within a year of Thornton's taking over the *Petard* the *Harvester* was sunk with the loss of many of her crew. HMS *Narcisissus* picked up 34 survivors. Her depth charges had forced the *U-444* to the surface, and *Harvester* then rammed her, causing the submarine to lodge beneath her hull before slipping clear. The same day the *Harvester* was hit by two torpedoes from the *U-432*, but her depth charges had damaged her attacker and an hour later she was forced to surface where she was rammed and sunk by the Fighting French

Navy destroyer *Aconit*.) Thornton worked the ship's company hard during training based at Scapa Flow, terrifying both officers and men.

The *Petard* began operations at the end of July 1942 when she was part of the naval escort for a convoy around the Cape of Good Hope to the Middle East. She sailed from Gourock to join the cruiser *Hawkins*, veteran of the First World War, the armed merchant cruiser *Ranpura* and the destroyer *Catterick* as escort to twelve large merchant ships. Next day they were reinforced by seven destroyers from Belfast.

The cargoes were destined for the hard-pressed Eighth Army, standing between FM Erwin Rommel's then triumphant Afrika Korps and the Suez Canal, regarded at the time as Britain's imperial lifeline. The long detour around Africa, taking fifty-four days, was necessary because the two European Axis powers, with clusters of air bases in Sicily, the toe of Italy and along the North African shore, made attempts to cross the Mediterranean from Gibraltar too costly.

At 5 a.m. on the first night at sea Lt Cdr Thornton called the radio direction-finding (RDF) mechanic Reg Crang to the bridge to tell him they were entering an area of heavy U-boat activity, and pounding his fist on the palm of his hand, he exclaimed, 'Crang I want a U-boat!' Noting this in a diary he kept in breach of wartime regulations, Reg Crang thought that his captain must be unaware of the limitations of RDF for submarine detection, adding, 'I just muttered that I would do my best and escaped from his awesome presence as soon as I could.'

On 1 August, in foggy conditions two days after sailing, trigger-happy gunners in merchant ships of the convoy shot down two Sunderland flying boats of RAF Coastal Command. Crang wrote in his diary, 'How awful. One crashed near us and burst into flames. We raced to the spot but there were no survivors, only wreckage and pitiful belongings of the crew. HMS *Ledbury* picked up a few survivors from the other Sunderland.'

A week later, the *Petard* crew were at action stations again when the RDF operators reported an echo, and seven depth charges were dropped without visible result. Later the same day Asdic, an echo-sounding device for locating submerged submarines, picked up echoes of several submarines, but no further action was taken. The name of this device came from the initial letters of the Allied Submarine Detective Investigation Committee of the First World War when it was invented, and it was later renamed Sonar. It was of little use in stormy weather, and its performance in picking up echoes from small surface targets was poor.

All twelve merchant ships reached harbour safely. The troops and supplies they landed arrived in Egypt at a critical time. Rommel's Afrika Korps was only 60 miles from the main eastern Mediterranean fleet base of Alexandria, poised to capture the Suez Canal.

Petard moored on a buoy in Port Said, close by the statue of Ferdinand de Lesseps, builder of the canal. Instead of carrying on to join the Eastern Fleet she became part of the 12th Destroyer Flotilla under the Commander-in-Chief, Levant. At this time German Stuka bombers from bases in Sicily, North Africa, Italy and Greece, had radically changed the naval situation in the Mediterranean. In December 1940 the Royal Navy had quickly established dominance over the Italian Navy when twenty-one torpedo bombers from the carrier *Illustrious* sank three battleships and damaged others at anchor in Taranto harbour. (This attack was much admired by Adm Isoruku Yamamato of Japan, who visited Taranto and later commanded the attack on Pearl Harbor.) Further heavy losses were inflicted on the Italian fleet in the Battle of Cape Matapan in March 1941, a triumph shared with Mavis Batey of Bletchley Park who decoded Enigma signals about a plan for heavy Italian warships to intercept an Allied convoy. But in April Hitler intervened to stiffen his Italian ally. His troops invaded Yugoslavia and Greece, backed by massed formations of Stuka dive-bombers of Fliegerkorps X, trained for attacks on shipping. The 50,000 British forces sent to help Greece were forced to withdraw to Crete, evacuated by the Navy under cover of night.

Ultra intelligence advised that the Germans then planned to take Crete by airborne invasion, information of little operational use because the British forces opposing them faced overwhelming numbers, even though the Navy sank or turned back ships carrying German reinforcements.

Finally, at the end of May 1941 the Navy rescued 34,000 troops from Crete under a ferocious battering from Stuka dive-bombers. The battleship *Warspite* had been badly damaged, and the cruisers *Fiji*, *Gloucester*, *Orion* and *Dido*, and the destroyers *Kelly*, *Kashmir*, *Hereward* and *Greyhound*, were all sunk or severely damaged.

So the fleet that *Petard* joined in August 1942, based on Alexandria, was much reduced; just a few cruisers, two destroyer flotillas and smaller craft.

Besides the numerous Stuka bomber squadrons Hitler had also diverted fifteen U-boats from the Atlantic to the Mediterranean in hopes of preventing

British warships from intercepting Rommel's supplies to North Africa. The loss of many of his supply ships was to continue to cripple Rommel throughout the desert campaign.

The *Petard*'s first call to action in these heavily disputed waters came at 4 a.m. on 24 September 1942 when she was ordered to hasten at top speed to join the cruisers *Orion* and *Arethusa*, along with destroyers *Pakenham*, *Paladin*, *Javelin*, *Kelvin* and others, to intercept an enemy invasion force reported to be heading for Cyprus. The report turned out to be false, and *Petard* was ordered back to Port Said just as three Ju 88 torpedo bombers were sighted. The destroyers laid a smokescreen to cover the cruisers, and then cut back through the smoke to engage the aircraft. The destroyers all fired salvoes, and the Junkers flew away.

During the next month the ship took part in weekly fleet manoeuvres. On 23 October the *Petard*'s Asdics located a U-boat just off the North African shore, and made depth-charge attacks. But the U-boat escaped and all contact was lost. Not far away the Battle of El Alamein, the turning point of the land war, was beginning. Reg Crang confided to his diary, 'When darkness fell the desert sky was lit by an explosion of gun-fire, a mighty barrage that must be a prelude to the long awaited assault by our army.'

A week after that came the most spectacular and tragic episode in the story of HMS *Petard*'s many actions. Soon after dawn on 30 October, a Sunderland flying boat reported a radar contact, possibly a submarine, in position 31 degrees 47 North, 33 degrees 24 East, about halfway between Port Said and Tel Aviv. The destroyers *Petard*, *Pakenham*, *Dulverton* and *Hurworth* were ordered to search. Meanwhile,

while these destroyers were racing at top speed from Port Said, the destroyer *Hero* intercepted the signals from 20 miles away and began a square search of the sighting area at 8.30 a.m. without making contact. Just under four hours later she was joined by the other destroyers, and shortly after that a Wellesley aircraft from 47 Squadron, RAF, joined the search. Its crew sighted a periscope and the outline of a submarine beneath the surface some five miles from the *Pakenham*, the nearest destroyer. The plane dropped a stick of three depth charges set to explode at a depth of 25 ft ahead of the swirl made by the submarine as it dived, but there was no sign of them causing damage, and the plane fired two white Very lights to indicate the position.

The destroyers approached at 31 knots, reducing to 15 knots as they reached the position, and the flotilla leader in the *Pakenham* organised them in a box search. This involved part of the force maintaining a ring around the area while other ships were poised to attack with depth charges when Asdic picked up signs of underwater movement.

For nearly half an hour, one of the *Petard*'s Asdic operators Jack Hall recalled, he and his colleagues listened intently for a tell-tale ping, but none came. The weather was fair with a wind blowing force 1–2 from the north-west. The Admiralty report on the hunt said that Asdic conditions were good. However, in his account written twenty years later former Sub Lt Connell said Asdic conditions were bad, favouring the U-boat. The sea water was disturbed by varying density and temperature bands and aggravated by freshwater discharges from the Nile Delta.

The search went on for nearly an hour before the

Asdic hut in the *Dulverton* reported a contact. *Petard* led the attack with eight depth charges at 1257 hr. They were fired from the after part of the ship, flying high in the air before dropping into the sea about 100 yd away. Then nothing could be seen for several seconds, the length of time depending on the depth the charges were set to detonate, and the explosion followed by huge fountains of water. As the water settled the crew were disappointed to see no signs of success, such as oil and U-boat debris. *Dulverton* then attacked with ten depth charges and five minutes later *Petard* loosed another ten depth charges. As she was going into this second attack the *Petard* crew heard a heavy explosion, apparently beneath the ship. It was also heard by the other ships, but there was no disturbance of water and shortly afterwards Jack Hall, in the Asdic hut, heard a hissing sound. This contact occupied the *Petard* crew and two of the other ships for nearly an hour until the *Pakenham*, making a box search with the *Hero* around them, detected the pings of U-boat movement further west. Then it was realised that the explosion must have been caused by the U-boat's evasion apparatus known as SBT.

During the next hour *Petard*, with two other destroyers, held the outer ring while *Pakenham* made two attacks, dropping eight depth charges in each, and the *Hero* dropped six depth charges.

An hour later in another series of attacks *Pakenham* dropped eight depth charges, the *Hurworth* ten. The *Hero* followed, dropping five depth charges in one attack and six in a second.

Another half-hour passed before *Dulverton* picked up a further contact and made an attack with ten depth charges, followed by eight, and *Pakenham* put in an eight depth-charge attack. But when the surface turbulence settled there was still no sign of success.

Late in the afternoon the *Hero*'s steering gear broke down. *Petard* relieved her in the ring while *Pakenham*, with only eight depth charges left, became directing ship. Over the next hour only the *Dulverton* took action, firing eight more depth charges. By this time the light was failing and many in *Petard*'s crew feared the elusive U-boat had made its escape, but A/PO Eric Sellars in the Asdic hut told Lt Cdr Thornton that he thought the U-boat was below 500 ft, the maximum setting on Royal Navy depth charges. He suggested stuffing soap into the holes in the depth-charge primers so that water pressure would build up more slowly and the charges would sink deeper before exploding.

AB Francis Cauldwell got to work with a bar of soap, and at 1842 hr *Petard* loosed ten soaped depth charges. It seemed a long wait for the explosions, but they came and the trick worked. The hunted U-boat moved and firm Asdic contact was regained.

During the next hour *Dulverton* made two attacks with ten depth charges in each, and having no more depth charges left, she was relieved by the *Hurworth*. Another silent hour went by before the *Hurworth* responded to an Asdic ping with five depth charges set to explode at various depths down to 250 ft.

Aboard the *Petard* just after 2200 hr PO Sellars reported a contact moving at 3 knots, and the *Petard* took up position to attack with five depth charges set to sandwich the U-boat between explosions above and below. The ship moved into her attacking speed of 18 knots, her course adjusted to allow for the U-boat's course, speed and the falling rate of the depth charges through the water after discharge from traps and throwers.

To the *Petard*'s crew, after nearly ten hours at action stations, the interval between firing and explosions seemed an eternity. When they came, the darkness of the night made the eruptions and whiteness of cascading water close to the ship seem devastating. Afterwards came deep silence except for the rising wind and the slap of waves. But this time the last depth charges had hit their mark. There was a smell of diesel fuel and shouts from the Asdic hut that they could hear a submarine blowing its tanks. Then came an eruption of white water at about 1,000 yd on the ship's port side. The bridge ordered the 36-in searchlight to be brought into play, but before the powerful beam was focused, Yeoman of Signals Robert Chapman used a port signal lamp to light up a conning tower with what looked like a white horse painted on it. Seconds later the searchlight's powerful beam, and a searchlight from the *Hurworth*, illuminated white figures emerging from the conning tower. They were scurrying along the casing towards the gun tower or jumping into the sea.

Lt Cdr Thornton ordered all armament to open fire, but the U-boat was too close for the 4-in B and X guns, and the *Petard* was briefly turned to allow B gun to fire a 4-in shell. It passed completely through the conning tower before exploding. After that only the pom-pom and one of the port oerlikons could be depressed low enough to open fire, and pom-pom shells and bullets hit the submarine casing and blew more holes in the conning tower. The oerlikon gunner, John Mackness, stood on a wooden platform specially made for him because his lack of height made depressing the gun difficult. He told the author from his Gosport home, fifty-five years later, 'I gave the conning tower a fair drumming.' The *Hurworth* also blasted the U-boat with pom-pom and oerlikon fire.

Seeing that the U-boat was stopped and its crew were abandoning their ship, Lt Anthony Fasson, standing by the captain on the bridge, rang the cease fire bells. He knew that the captain was intent on boarding a U-boat before it sank from depth-charge damage or scuttling charges. They had talked frequently about tactics for seizing an enemy coding machine and cipher documents. As the U-boat was forced to the surface Lt Cdr Thornton shouted orders to the gunnery officer, Sub Lt Connell, to leave his gun-directing position and go down to the forecastle to prepare to lead a boarding party.

By this time, 2245 hr, *Petard* was hove to with the *U-559* low in the water about 60 yd away on the port side, down by the bows in a roughening sea. Outside the beam of light from the *Petard* all was darkness. The *Dulverton* circled to ward off attack by any other U-boats.

As Connell reached the forecastle, the faces and arms of the U-boat crew showed up in the searchlight beam as they swam towards them, and the captain shouted to him to dive over the side and swim to the U-boat. Connell began disrobing his flash protective clothing as a boarding party gathered. Among them was AB Colin Grazier, who was stripping off his overall and saying he would swim across with the sub-lieutenant. Then Lt Fasson scrambled out of the darkness from the starboard side aft where he had been organising the sea boat for lowering. After his discussions with his skipper on plans for boarding a U-boat to capture the ciphers he had trained a boarding party in tactics which included throwing a chain across an open conning tower to prevent it from being closed. This was the very opportunity to put it all into action, and he was not going to miss it. Already capless, he was kicking off half-wellingtons and tearing off his uniform as he changed Connell's instructions. Because Fasson was taking over the task of swimming to the U-boat, Connell instead was to go aft to complete the lowering of the whaler and to get it alongside the U-boat at top speed. Then Fasson dived over the side and swam to the U-boat, followed closely by AB Grazier.

In the darkness, amid excitement and confusion it was thought that canteen assistant Tommy Brown had also stripped off and plunged into the sea from the waist of the ship, swimming after them. That became part of the legend about his brave deed. However, at a naval inquiry ordered by Commander-in-Chief, Levant eight months later, he was asked 'How did you board the U-boat?' He replied, 'I got on board just forward of the whaler on the port side when the deck was level with the conning tower. I got on the conning tower.' His evidence continued,

> I first helped to make fast – three or four lines snapped until we made fast with a manila (thick rope) passed from the ship. I then went down below. The First Lieutenant was down there with A/B Grazier. I carried a lot of books up and tried to make a line fast (from the top of the conning tower to below) so I could get more up, and then left the others to do this and went down below again.
>
> The First Lieutenant was using a machine-gun to smash open cabinets in the commanding officer's cabin. He then tried some of the keys hanging behind

the door and opened a drawer, taking out some confidential books which he gave me. I put them at the bottom of the hatch, and after more books were found in a big cabinet just above the C.O.'s bunk I took them and another lot up.

Asked about the situation inside the U-boat Brown answered,

> The lights were out – the First Lieutenant had a torch. The water was not very high but rising gradually all the time. When I came up the last time it was about two feet deep. There was a hole just forward of the conning tower through which water was pouring. As I went down through the conning tower compartment I felt it pouring down my back. Water was also coming in where plates were stove in on either side of the conning tower.

Brown added that on his third visit below the first lieutenant was trying to break some apparatus from a bulkhead in the main control room.

> We got it away from the bulkhead, but it was held fast by a number of wires and we gave up. The water was getting deeper and I told the First Lieutenant that they were all shouting on deck for us to leave. He gave me some more books and I took these up, and they were passed into the whaler.
>   When I looked down the hatch again the water was coming over the upper deck. I saw Grazier and then the First Lieutenant also appeared at the bottom of the hatch. I shouted 'You had better come up' twice, and they had just started when the submarine

started to sink very quickly. I managed to jump off and was picked up by the whaler.

AB Kenneth Lacroix told the inquiry that he boarded the U-boat from the *Petard*'s port quarter, and helped to make a line fast to the conning tower. Then he joined Brown at the top of the conning tower and fixed a line to pull up books. He went on,

> I then pulled up some books from the control tower, waited for the whaler to come alongside and then passed on the books. The First Lieutenant shouted up 'Go carefully with this instrument. It is very delicate'. It was made fast to a line for us to haul up. I went inside the control room (the conning tower one) and when the box came level with me the First Lieutenant shouted up again, saying that we were hauling it up too fast as it was very delicate.
>
> When the order came to abandon ship water was pouring in the top and I did not see the box again. I was the last on the conning tower, and water was pouring down and as I climbed the last two rungs of the ladder I had to pull against it to get out. There was still suction as I swam away and was picked up by the whaler. There was a wounded man on top of the conning tower.

AB G.W. MacFarlane told the inquiry that he boarded the U-boat when she was alongside the *Petard*'s port side, adding 'I went on to the conning tower with the navigating officer and helped with the confidential books. Later we hauled a box up to the top of the conning tower. I gathered it was a very delicate instrument as the First Lieutenant shouted up that we were to go carefully with it. The order came to abandon ship and I had to leave it as water was rising above the conning tower. I never realised the ship was sinking. It happened very suddenly.' (MacFarlane later transferred to a submarine which was lost on operations.)

Lt Spens-Black RN, the navigating officer, told the inquiry that he boarded the U-boat as she came down the port side abreast of the forward torpedo tubes. He then assisted with securing the manila, and then went to the conning tower where they were hauling up confidential books. He went on, 'The First Lieutenant had shouted "Box coming up. Be careful as it looks to me as if it is important." We were hauling it up as the boat started going down. I shouted "Abandon ship" and we had to leave the box.' Asked how water was getting into the U-boat, he replied, 'I have no first hand information but the First Lieutenant shouted up shortly after he had gone below that she was holed forward. I could see no water rushing in, but the books were dry when they reached the top of the hatch.'

Recollections of what could be seen from the *Petard*'s decks in pitch darkness save for the beams from both destroyers' searchlights that stressful night have become confused and varied after the passing of so many years, but judging from the evidence given at the inquiry the *Petard* could have been right alongside the *U-559* only briefly, unknown to Connell and his boarding party; she must have stood off again quickly because the U-boat was being tossed about in the mounting waves. Connell's whaler was lowered at the stern of the starboard side, the blind side, and she had to be rowed around the ship in choppy water before reaching the U-boat. In his account Connell made no mention of this, nor of the men who took the opportunity to jump aboard the U-boat directly from the *Petard*. He also wrote that Tommy Brown swam to the U-boat. Oddly, he was not called to give evidence at the inquiry.

Connell told of reaching the U-boat after being hampered by Germans from the U-boat hanging on to the gunwales, and the battering the whaler had to withstand alongside the U-boat in choppy sea with the casing of the U-boat awash with bows low in the water. Connell described his surprise at finding Tommy Brown clinging to the outside ladder of the conning tower, and related how he ordered Brown not to go down again, but to shout down to Fasson and Grazier that they should come up at once. He told of how he tried to climb the conning tower himself as the U-boat sank, and had to be pulled back into the whaler from the swirling water. Yet he made no mention of the other three members of the *Petard*'s crew who were around the conning tower at the time, one of them mentioned in dispatches.

Connell's whaler pulled Tommy Brown out of the water, and then lingered on the spot as turbulence settled, with the sailors repeatedly calling the names of Fasson and Grazier. A German who had been lying wounded at the top of the conning tower was picked up, but there was no sign of the two British sailors. By that time a second whaler must have picked up the three others and taken them back to the *Petard*, while Connell's whaler was still hoping to find Fasson and Grazier.

At his home in Bournemouth, former AB Mervyn Romeril recalled seeing the starboard whaler cleared with the boarding party, 'It was pitch dark and we could only see what happened in the searchlight beams. As I was the starboard look-out the super-structure would have prevented me seeing what happened on the port side. The *Petard* was moving slowly all the time. Some of us were helping pull up the German survivors who had swum to the scrambling nets we had thrown over the side. They hadn't the strength to climb up by themselves in their wet uniforms.'

In Witham, Essex, former LS Ted Saunders remembered the confusing scene, 'When we get together with old shipmates at the HMS *Petard* Association we seem to have a variety of different recollections of what happened. I don't recollect that the *Petard* went alongside, or that the second whaler was lowered. I saw Fasson and Grazier dive in and swim towards the U-boat, but only heard that Tommy Brown had followed them in swimming to the U-boat.'

It is generally agreed that the *Petard*, her sides still draped with scrambling nets up which some of the enemy had scrambled to safety and captivity, finally went alongside Connell's whaler and after pausing for her to be fixed to the davits the whaler was hoisted back aboard as the ship got under way. The searchlight extinguished, *Petard* moved at speed away from the area.

The Admiralty's report of the operation to sink the *U-559* says that both the *Petard*'s whalers were lowered, and it has to be assumed that it was the port whaler that picked up Lt Spens-Black, AB Lacroix and AB MacFarlane.

During the ten hours the hunt lasted, the *U-559* covered about thirty miles, zigzagging underwater. An Admiralty report on the *U-559* sinking concluded 'The battle was won largely by persistence.'

The *U-559*'s commander, Korvettleutnant Hans Heidtmann, had given the order to abandon ship when the submarine reached the surface. He was among the three officers and eleven ratings of the U-boat's crew to survive. The German engineering officer confirmed that he had opened the seacocks before obeying the order to abandon ship, expecting the U-boat to sink immediately.

The U-boat crew said they had counted 288 depth-charge explosions during the hunt, but the total dropped in eighteen attacks was 150. Other ammunition expenditure by the *Petard* was listed at 1 4-in shell, 114 pom-pom shells and 79 oerlikon rounds. The *Petard*'s last depth charges had staved in plates on the U-boat's starboard quarter. By that time the air in the U-boat was intolerable, as though the oxygen had run out, and the captain ordered the ship to surface.

What looked like a white horse on the conning tower was in fact a donkey, a touch of Teutonic humour as the crew believed they had eaten donkey sliced as salami when based in Greece. The *U-559* had been among the first U-boats sent into the Mediterranean, and she had left Messina in Sicily on this her tenth and last cruise on 29 September. On previous cruises she had sunk the Australian destroyer *Parramata* and several supply ships and also fired torpedoes unsuccessfully at a destroyer screen. Her last cruise had been fruitless and without incident until she was hunted and sunk.

Diarist Reg Crang told the author that he understood that Fasson and Thornton had their own plan for rapid boarding of a surfaced U-boat, and he believed that Fasson must have carried the torch and machine-gun with him in a waterproof bag as he swam to the U-boat. He noted the events of that dramatic day and night in his secret diary:

Asdic contact was intermittent, but all four destroyers dropped patterns of depth charges in turn. The ocean shook violently again and again, with huge eruptions of sea water surging into the air. There was intense excitement among the crew for we all felt confident that our prey could not escape from this fierce bombardment. But no evidence of damage came to the surface, and as hours slipped by our spirits began to drop.

When darkness fell the *Pakenham* and *Hurworth* left to search another area, leaving *Petard* in charge with the Hunt class destroyer *Dulverton* in support. With asdic contact lost for long periods we began to get disheartened.

However, at about 2300 the alarm bells rang again. I rushed on deck to see the U-boat caught in the searchlight. It was a frightening sight, a dramatic first view of the enemy. Someone shouted stand-by to ram. I began to blow up my lifebelt although I knew it had a bad leak.

Our pom-poms and oerlikons opened fire on the conning tower plastering it with shells. The U-boat was clearly in a helpless position so we drew alongside. It was awe-inspiring to be so close to the enemy. Survivors began to jump in the water and swim towards us. We lowered rope ladders and netting to allow them to scramble aboard. Meanwhile, a boat was launched to take a boarding party across to the U-boat. Before it got there three of our crew had stripped naked and swam across.

The survivors started to scramble up the ropes but they were shaken and it was an ordeal. One with terrible stomach wounds got stuck unable to climb further. His comrades tried to help him, but he slipped off and drifted away. I leant over and seized one man, pulling him in with great effort. I was thrilled to get a German in my hands and felt like shaking him to bits. But we pushed them all aft, many of them trembling from their ordeal. But they recovered quite quickly, some becoming cheerful and even arrogant.

But soon we learnt of our own casualties, a tragic loss that left us all speechless. The boarding party led by Gordon Connell had come back without Tony Fasson and Colin Grazier. They had gone down with the U-boat which sank so suddenly that they were unable to scramble out of the conning tower. The First Lieutenant had descended into the control room to rescue documents and secret coding material. This had been handed to Colin Grazier and then on to Tommy Brown who clung on to the U-boat casing while passing the vital material to the boarding party.

This party had just started to jump aboard when the U-boat sank with the two gallant men unaware that disaster was upon them. Tommy Brown and Gordon Connell were able to scramble into the sea boat to return with the devastating news.

Jimmy, as we all knew him, was a real man's man, already a legend on the ship. Handsome and arrogant, but deadly efficient, he was admired by everyone. He was ready with a smile and a joke for the humblest O.D. We cannot imagine there's a finer First Lieutenant in the Navy.

As HMS *Petard* sped from the area a signal with a guarded message was sent, indicating the capture of documents, and she was ordered to sail for Haifa at full speed, escorted by *Dulverton*. There they were met by naval intelligence officers who sent the captured documents by courier to London where they were presumed to have been passed on urgently to Bletchley Park, the British code-breaking centre. Meanwhile, the German prisoners were disembarked, and the *Petard*'s crew, divided into two watches, were given 48 hours' leave, each watch in turn. Some of them visited Jerusalem, the River Jordan, the Sea of Galilee and the Dead Sea.

Lt Cdr Thornton busied himself, making recommendations for awards to his crew. Citing Lt Fasson he wrote, 'When the U-boat surfaced and surrendered he went over the side from the forecastle and boarded with great dash. He stayed below working in darkness with water rising, knowing the sub to be holed. He continued to get out books and instruments until the sub sank. He gave his life in his eagerness to get vital information.'

His citation for Grazier read, 'This excellent young seaman followed the First Lieutenant over the side from the forecastle and with him boarded the U-boat in the shortest possible time. He stayed below working in darkness with water rising and knowing the sub to be holed until too late get out, thus giving his life in his eagerness to get vital information.'

About Brown he wrote, 'He unhesitatingly jumped on to the U-boat to assist Lieut. Fasson. He went below three times in darkness to bring up books knowing the U-boat was holed in two places steadily taking water. He was a fine example of coolness and courage in a hazardous situation, more especially in one so young (16 years).'

When details of the sinking of *U-559* and Thornton's recommendations for awards reached the Admiralty it was decided that Fasson and Grazier had shown bravery worthy of the Victoria Cross. But there were deep worries about the interest the posthumous awards of two VCs might arouse, and the likelihood that enemy intelligence might enquire more deeply into the circumstances. Their Lordships found the excuse that the VC was intended for the bravest deeds carried out in the face of the enemy and in this case the bravery had been shown after military action was completed. So they recommended posthumous awards of the George Cross, the highest bravery awards for civilians.

A minute of the Honours and Awards Committee noted that the question of the correct awards for Fasson, Grazier and Brown presented some difficulty, while the actions of Fasson and Grazier were clearly up to George Cross/Victoria Cross standard: 'They went below in a submarine that they knew to be sinking in an endeavour to obtain information of vital importance: the service can hardly be called a "suicide job" since they must have hoped to survive to bring up the information. They certainly knew the risk was very great and they took it deliberately for the sake of the information. Also in estimating their gallantry the fact is relevant that they stuck to the job, though the rising water must have shown them that the risk was every moment getting greater and greater.'

The minute went on to say that an informal inquiry to the secretary of the George Cross Committee elicited the opinion that the committee would not consider it because the George Cross was instituted for gallantry in civil defence against air raids and circumstances arising out of them. It concluded by submitting that agreement on these awards should be put to the George Cross Committee as strongly as possible, and this was done. The main objection came from the Treasury

Committee appointed to vet awards. They requested an explanation, commenting, 'The George Cross is not instituted with a view to rewarding actions of this kind, immediately following combat with the enemy.'

The George Cross recommendations sparked much correspondence, some via radio signals. A cable to the Commander-in-Chief, Levant, on 1 April 1943 from J.P. Droop, head of the Honours and Awards Committee, said that the George Cross Committee believed the award of the George Cross to be inappropriate. It should be regarded as service in action. Would they recommend the Victoria Cross? A reply dated 8 April said, 'It is specially requested that nothing be published that may suggest we recovered anything of value from the U-boat.' A signal later the same day added, 'Regret I am unable to recommend the Victoria Cross. The U-boat had been abandoned by the enemy and was alongside the Petard. It was hoped the George Cross would be appropriate for a very brave action by Lieut Fasson and Able Seaman Grazier in boarding at night and remaining below in a flooding submarine and continuing the salvage of very valuable paper and instruments.' His last comment demonstrated some impatience: 'Failing this I recommend a posthumous Mention in Despatches.'

At this stage the Director of Naval Intelligence intervened to classify all the correspondence 'Most Secret', and emphasised that 'knowledge of the salvage of documents or instruments from a U-boat must be restricted to the barest minimum of people even in the Admiralty, and on no account should such an episode be made public or promulgated to anyone whose official duties do not necessitate the knowledge.'

This was followed up by a letter from the First Lord

of the Admiralty to Sir Robert Knox at the Treasury, arguing for the top civilian award because combat had ceased but the gallantry was equivalent to any in action. His letter ended, 'This question, since it deals with getting vital information from the enemy, should be treated as Most Secret.'

J.P. Droop, resisted an attempt to reduce the award to Tommy Brown to the British Empire Medal by stating in a letter dated 19 July, 'He went down three times to bring up books, etc. When he went down the third time people on the deck were shouting. The U-boat sank just as he came up and he jumped and was picked up from the sea, and the Admiralty view is that the courage he showed was of a higher grade than would have qualified for the BEM.'

While this correspondence went on, the *London Gazette* of 12 January 1943 announced that Lt Cdr Mark Thornton DSC, RN was to be a Companion of the Distinguished Service Order for his command of HMS *Petard* during a successful attack on an enemy submarine. On 23 March 1943 the *London Gazette* announced the following awards 'for skill and enterprise while serving in HMS Petard in a successful attack on an enemy submarine': the DSC to Lt David Dunbar Nasmith RN, the DSM to Yeoman of Signals Randell Chapman and LS Trevor Tipping, and mentions in dispatches to Midshipman Peter Thomas Alleyne Goddard RN and Signalman Kenneth Hannay.

It was not until the following August that Sir Henry Markham sent a final letter from Treasury chambers to say that the controversy over the George Cross awards had ended in agreement. They were approved by the King on 9 September, and published on 14 September 1943. The *London Gazette* announced the posthumous awards of the George Cross to Lt Anthony Blair Fasson and AB Colin Grazier for 'outstanding bravery and steadfast devotion to duty in the face of danger', but gave no other details. It also announced the award of the George Medal to junior canteen assistant Thomas William Brown for 'bravery and devotion to duty in the face of danger'. The next edition of the *London Gazette* printed a correction, giving Fasson's full name as Lt Francis Anthony Blair Fasson.

Capt Stevens, the 12th Destroyer Flotilla commander aboard the *Pakenham*, was awarded a bar to his Distinguished Service Order. The recommendation, classified Most Secret, from the *Petard*'s captain, Lt Cdr Mark Thornton, DSO, DSC, RN, read 'The destruction of the *U-559* on 30 October, 1942, was principally due to his skill, persistence and direction through this long and successful hunt.' On recommendations from Capt Stevens the captains of the *Pakenham* and the *Hero* were awarded the Distinguished Service Cross. Capt Stevens's own recommendation for an award to the *Petard*'s captain indicates that he was poorly informed about what actually happened during the *Petard*'s encounter with the *U-559*. It read, 'When the U-boat surfaced the Petard engaged her and subsequently proceeded alongside, boomed her and took her in tow before she sank – an outstanding exhibition of seamanship which resulted in the capture of many confidential books.'

Other recommendations for awards by the *Petard*'s captain were duly given: Lt Robert Eliot Frank de Pass RN, the torpedo officer, 'This clever young officer was of the greatest assistance to me. He showed vision and understanding in interpreting the situation. His enthusiasm throughout the hunt was a considerable factor in its success'; A/PO Eric Sellars, 'For most of the long hunt he was operating the Asdic set. He is a first class MSD (chief Asdic operator)'; AB Kenneth Vivian Lacroix, 'He was chosen by the MSD to relieve him when he was ordered to rest. He stayed at the top of the conning tower trying to get the last lot away until water almost sucked him under as the U-boat sank'; AB Francis James Cauldwell, 'Throughout the operation he showed greet keenness and alacrity working on depth charges. Seeing the necessity of passing a line he at once jumped overboard and swam to the U-boat.' (The captain was wrong about him swimming to the U-boat. Cauldwell told the inquiry that he jumped from the *Petard* directly on to the *U-559*.)

Two Distinguished Service Medals went to petty officers serving in the *Pakenham* and *Dulverton*, and three mentioned in dispatches awards went to crew members of the *Dulverton*, another three to the *Hurworth* and one to the *Hero*.

At sixteen, though claiming to be a year older, Tommy Brown was the youngest recipient of the George Medal. Despite his age he stayed with the *Petard* until she returned to Britain in 1944. Later, he was appointed the senior canteen assistant aboard the cruiser HMS *Belfast* (now a museum in the River Thames), and while she was being refitted for the Far East war in February 1945, Brown was sleeping at his nearby family home in Lily Gardens, Ridges Estate, attending aboard ship every day. Tommy Brown, then nineteen, and a four-year-old sister died when fire broke out in the early hours of 13 February 1945. His mother, three brothers and six other sisters escaped. His father, a Royal Engineer, had gone back from leave a week before. His mother, Margaret Brown, went to Buckingham Palace to receive

Tommy's George Medal from King George VI in July 1945. In 1985 the family presented his George Medal, five campaign medals and a clock presented to him by the NAAFI, to the museum at NAAFI headquarters at Amesbury, Wiltshire.

Lt Cdr Thornton sent a German U-boat seaman's jacket to Walker's shipyard in Newcastle to honour a promise he had made to the shipyard workers that he would send them trophies of the *Petard*'s success.

The delicate instrument that Lt Fasson was so intent on capturing undamaged, delaying escape too long, must have been the *U-559*'s Enigma machine. Tragically, he was not to know that far more valuable secret material was already safely in the *Petard*'s whaler, and that obtaining the Enigma machine would have been of comparatively little value, as Bletchley Park already had at least the one captured by HMS *Bulldog*. The *Petard*'s coup in capturing the *U-559* documents and cribs came after a costly ten-month gap in Britain's ability to read German U-boat signals traffic. But there were no headlines to cheer the people at home through this period of successive defeats and setbacks, and HMS *Petard* missed out on the fame she had earned.

With the captured material the scholars at Bletchley Park were able to break into the four-rotor Triton code, and from Sunday 13 December 1942, just six weeks after the *Petard*'s capture of the *U-559* material, much U-boat traffic was being read. The intelligence this provided through Ultra was to prove invaluable in winning the Battle of the Atlantic, then at its most critical stage in a momentous struggle with U-boat wolf-packs.

Eventual Allied victory depended on that success.

Chapter Five

Victory in the Battle of the Atlantic

The documents captured by HMS *Petard* included a current *Kurzsignalheft* (short signal book) and the 1942 *Wetterkurzschlussel* (short weather cipher). The first documents reached the eager code-breakers at Bletchley Park on 4 November, but the one they most urgently needed, the short weather cipher, was not passed on to Bletchley Park until 24 November, a loss of three weeks that has not been explained.

It was the capture of the 1940 *Kurzschlussel* cipher from the weather-ship *Muenchen* in May 1941 (reaching Bletchley Park three days later) that had helped the code-breakers to solve the three-rotor naval Enigma the Germans called 'Heimisch' (Home) after many months of sustained effort. From August 1941, this had great influence on the Atlantic battle. Losses of Allied ships had been reduced by diverting convoys while more U-boats were located and sunk. This advantage had come to an end with the introduction of a fourth rotor in new M4 Enigma machines, for use only on the U-boat Triton network. The machines were put into service on 1 February 1942, and had made Bletchley Park blind to U-boat signals for ten months as Atlantic shipping losses reached critical levels.

There had been immense anxiety for some time at Bletchley Park that the enormous advantage of reading much of the U-boat operational traffic might be coming to an end. These fears were confirmed in December 1941 when they found out about an imminent change to an Enigma machine with four rotors, for U-boats operating in the Atlantic and Mediterranean. This was learned through a mistake made by a U-boat radio operator. He had enciphered an unusually long message in a four-rotor Triton code, the methods for which he must have been under training, and began transmitting it before realising his error. He then re-enciphered the message in the current three-rotor Enigma key.

Using these two intercepts Bletchley experts were able to work out the wiring of a fourth rotor. But the complexities were enormous in solving the many times multiplied combinations involved, and there were practically no cribs during the ten months' blackout. It took twenty-six times longer to run a four-rotor crib through the three-rotor Bombes made available, and in any case there were insufficient Bombes for the current Luftwaffe and German Army traffic. But when Harold Keen, who headed Bombe production at the British Tabulating Machine Company, was consulted he used well-established electronic techniques to modify Bombes so that they were able to do twenty-six times as many tests as the normal three-wheel bombes in only twice the time. He knew from experience that he could safely drive the drums much faster.

When the first four-rotor Bombe became operational in June 1943, these earlier developments enabled Bletchley Park to solve the keys and read Triton traffic successfully on only three days before they broke the code with the *U-559* material. As code-breakers at Bletchley Park began studying this material, captured by HMS *Petard* far from the menace in the Atlantic, the biggest U-boat offensive was reaching a climax and was close to gaining the upper hand.

The second edition of the short weather cipher was precisely what the cryptanalysts had been hoping for. From this key document, when it finally reached them, they learned that the four-letter indicators for regular U-boat messages were the same as those used as three-letter indicators for weather messages except for one added letter. This meant that once a daily key was found for a weather message the four-rotor signals needed to be tested on the Bombes in only twenty-six positions to find the full key.

The Germans named their new M4 Enigma Triton after the son of Poseidon, the Greek ocean demigod who blew through a twisted sea shell to stir storms. Bletchley Park gave it the code name Shark. The vital key for the first decrypts of Shark signals was found on Sunday 13 December, just six weeks after the sinking of the *U-559*. It had taken constant work and thousands of Bombe runs before this success was achieved. Later that day, solutions to the hitherto impenetrable four-rotor Enigma messages between U-boats at sea and the U-boat Command started to emerge. Only an hour after the first decrypts were made intercepts of U-boat signals were sent to the Admiralty's Submarine Tracking Room. They revealed the positions of fifteen U-boats.

Convoys from the United States carrying supplies for their forces in North Africa began getting through without loss, evading the known positions of U-boat wolf-packs revealed by Ultra. It was estimated that reading Triton signals saved between 500,000 and 750,000 tons of shipping in December 1942 and January 1943 alone. In the first few days of 1943, Ultra located a wolf-pack of six U-boats lying in wait between the Azores and Madeira. Having none of his usual B-Dienst intelligence on this convoy, mainly organised by military signals, Doenitz knew nothing about it until a lone U-boat chanced upon the convoy, and signals for it to trail the convoy and orders gathering other U-boats into the area were decrypted at Bletchley Park.

A convoy of nine fully laden tankers designated TMI, escorted by the destroyer HMS *Havelock* and three corvettes, was ordered to divert sharply to the south, a route which would have avoided the U-boat ambushes by 100 miles. But the destroyer's captain, Cdr R.C. Boyle, unaware of the 'golden' source of the intelligence on which the detour was based, decided to maintain his original course rather than head for rougher weather he knew to be in the south, because of the imminent necessity of refuelling the Corvettes. That doom-laden decision was tragically followed by one of the occasional interruptions Bletchley Park suffered. The Germans changed the Triton setting at noon and Bletchley Park was unable to read further U-boat traffic for 48 hours, and there was a flurry of U-boat messages for the next three days. Before Ultra was restored seven tankers, totalling 55,000 tons and carrying 100,000 tons of badly needed fuel, were sunk – a 77 per cent loss and the highest proportion of any convoy lost throughout the war. But from then until the war ended Bletchley Park was able to read U-boat traffic on a nearly current basis.

At their conference in Casablanca in January 1943, Churchill made it clear to President Roosevelt that unless the U-boats could be overcome the war would be lost. Britain would face starvation, an invasion of mainland Europe could never be mounted and the Russians would be deprived of essential war supplies from their western allies. The transfer of escorts to protect North African invasion shipping had been one cause of a sharp increase in merchant ship losses and Churchill urged Roosevelt to redress this by agreeing that victory over the U-boats was to have absolute priority.

When America entered the war after their main fleet was devastated by the Japanese attack on Pearl Harbor, American Navy chiefs had argued against President Roosevelt's policy – agreed with Churchill – of giving priority to gaining victory in Europe first. They concentrated their strongest naval forces against Japan, while the brunt of the Atlantic battle was borne by the navies of Britain, Canada and other Allies.

America advised Britain on its breaking of the Japanese code they called 'Purple' and Britain shared Ultra intelligence with American chiefs. A United States intelligence team, led by New York lawyer Telford Taylor, joined Bletchley Park for a while and then set up an Enigma code-breaking team of their own in New York that employed many more Bombes and personnel than Bletchley Park.

Meanwhile, in the non-stop Atlantic battle the biggest advantage for the U-boat packs was a wide mid-Atlantic gap beyond the range of aircraft from both sides of the ocean. The RAF chief, ACM Sir Arthur Harris, stubbornly kept his bomber offensive against German industry as his top priority and under pressure released only twenty-four Liberators for the Atlantic battle. Their four engines gave them longer range than inadequate types like the Avro Hanson which had been carrying out ocean patrols. RAF Coastal Command also operated Sunderland flying boats.

The Air Staff, dominated by Harris, believed that the best form of attack against U-boats was to bomb their bases and the yards where they were built. In fact not one U-boat was destroyed by the heavy bombing of the U-boat pens on the French Atlantic coast, but the RAF took heavy losses (100 heavy bombers in the first five months of 1943 alone) in pressing home attacks. They hit the pens with 15,000 tons of bombs, but the massive reinforced concrete structures were all but indestructible.

The fact that U-boats, particularly when hunting in wolf-packs, depended on radio to organise their combined attacks provided a rich harvest for Ultra when the daily Triton key could be found, which happened on most days.

A single U-boat or long-range Focke-Wulfe Condor reconnaissance plane would locate a convoy, and its composition, course and speed, number of ships and type of escort would be transmitted to U-boat headquarters at Lorient on the French Atlantic coast. The operations room there would then transmit instructions for all U-boats in the area to assemble, sometimes as many as twenty for a large convoy. As each U-boat was contacted it would signal acknowledgement and give its position. These signals were all in the German Navy's version of Enigma (Schlussel M), and these messages were much more secure than other signals.

About this time analysis of German signals traffic at Bletchley Park clearly indicated that B-Dienst, Bletchley's German counterpart, was reading British convoy codes, but the new code was not in general use until July 1943 because of the time it took to distribute new code books to distant parts of the world.

As the U-boat maximum effort reached a crescendo in the opening months of 1943 the Submarine Tracking Room, by then deep within a bombproof concrete bunker behind the Admiralty, was receiving a steady service of decrypts from the Triton cipher. U-boats were located, orders from U-boat Command were known and countered and convoys were re-routed. Sinkings of merchant ships were halved in January and February from the high figures of the previous two months.

Following a feeble performance by the pocket battleships *Admiral Hipper* and *Lutzow* (formerly *Deutschland*) against a convoy to Russia escorted by six destroyers in the first days of 1943 a furious Hitler sacked Grand Adm Raeder, and made Gossadmiral Doenitz commander-in-chief of the German Navy. He retained personal command of the U-boats, and U-boat headquarters was moved with him to Berlin. At the same time he noticed that B-Dienst transcripts of the British convoy codes showed that Allied reports on U-boats and other information transmitted to convoys and their escorts were disturbingly accurate. He ordered an inquiry into the security of the naval Enigma. The inquiry by Adm Kurt Fricke reported that there was no doubt that the Enigma system was unbreakable. The accuracy of Allied intelligence was put down to observations by fishing vessels and dockland spies. In his postwar memoirs, published in 1958, Adm Doenitz wrote 'Our ciphers were checked and re-checked to make sure they were unbreakable, and on each occasion the Head of the Naval Intelligence Service at Naval High Command adhered to his opinion that it would be impossible for the enemy to decipher them. And to this

HMS *Petard* during her first commission.

Petard's crew at Port Said, October 1942. The ship's name is held by sixteen-year-old NAAFI assistant Tommy Brown who won the George Medal.

Depth-charge explosions during long hunt for the *U-559*.

Another depth charge explodes. Both these photographs were taken from the *Petard*'s bridge.

The *U-559* forced to surface after nightfall.

The Italian flag captured from the *Uarsciek*, shown to cheering crowds as *Petard* entered Malta's Grand Harbour.

Lt Antony Fasson, George Cross.

AB Colin Grazier, George Cross.

Gen Eisenhower aboard *Petard* off the Sicilian invasion beaches.

Lt Cdr Rupert Egan introduces the ship's company for a BBC broadcast to families.

The Japanese super-submarine *I-27* manoeuvring to ram the crippled British destroyer *Paladin*.

The *Petard*'s seventh torpedo hits and destroys the *I-27*.
(All the above courtesy of Lt Cdr Robert de Pass)

HMS *Petard* at speed during her second commission.

Tank transporter stuck on Morib beach, D-Day.
(Courtesy of Stanley Skinner)

The Japanese destroyer *Kamikaze* flies the Royal Navy's white ensign over the rising sun flag of Japan when it surrenders charts of minefields to the *Petard*, 2 September 1945. (Stephen Harper)

A party from the *Petard* ready to land to secure lighthouses in Sumatra during the second commission. (Stephen Harper)

day, so far as I know, we are not certain whether or not the enemy did succeed in breaking our ciphers during the war.'

Soon after moving U-boat headquarters to Berlin Doenitz ordered his many U-boats to make a maximum effort to cut Britain's Atlantic lifelines. Sinkings of Allied ships climbed from twenty-nine (203,000 tons) in January to ninety-five (627,000 tons) in March. This was the most savage phase of the Atlantic battle when evasive routing was made impossible because of the size of the U-boat packs spread across the ocean. That rate of loss was almost double the rate new merchant ships were being built, while the sinking of nineteen U-boats represented only half the forty new U-boats ready for action. The daily average of U-boats operating in the Atlantic rose from 92 in January to 111 in April. During the rest of 1943 an average 116 U-boats were at sea every day.

As already noted this maximum effort was based on calculations by the U-boat Command that by sinking 800,000 tons monthly they would force Britain, faced with starvation, to sue for peace. This figure appeared to be well within their reach. The Germans seemed on the point of victory in the Atlantic, the most decisive battle of the war.

Doenitz made full use of intelligence supplied by B-Dienst, which had succeeded in penetrating British naval codes used to organise and route convoys. German cryptanalysts were reading British convoy codes (though they never broke naval operational signals) long before Bletchley succeeded in reading more than a few of theirs, and at this decisive stage of the Atlantic war they were reading 80 per cent of this British signals traffic. This meant that the U-boat High

Command was able to plot the route of many of the Atlantic convoys.

This information guided Adm Doenitz in positioning his U-boats for the biggest convoy battle of the war, in March 1943. He concentrated thirty-nine U-boats to intercept two convoys which sailed from Halifax, Nova Scotia to Liverpool – a slow convoy of fifty-two ships and a fast one of twenty-five. The fast convoy met up with them first and lost eight ships in as many hours. Then the two convoys joined together so that their escorts could combine. A running battle lasted three days and a total of twenty-one ships, totalling 140,000 tons, were sunk, four of them by one U-boat, the *U-338*. Only one U-boat was sunk. If this success could have been maintained Adm Doenitz's aim of cutting Britain's lifeline would have been achieved.

During this critical period, when Doenitz had nearly 400 U-boats engaged in the heaviest convoy battles of the war, Bletchley Park was having problems resulting from Doenitz's command for tighter Enigma security. U-boat operators had been ordered to take greater care against repetitions and other mistakes, and the menus seeking the daily keys for Triton became harder to find. During ten days in January 1943, no Enigma settings were worked out, and there were also none solved between 10 and 17 February. Despite these bad patches the *Petard*'s capture of the short weather code book resulted in Bletchley Park solving Shark traffic for ninety out of ninety-nine days between 13 December 1942 and 10 March 1943. Then a new Enigma weather cipher, much more complicated than the earlier two, came into effect, and Bletchley Park was deprived of weather cribs. The director of naval intelligence advised that the change would blind Bletchley Park again for a considerable period. However, the short signal book, also lifted by the *Petard* crew from the *U-559*, enabled cryptanalysts in Hut 8 to find cribs among sighting reports sent by U-boats in contact with convoys. For 87 of the 112 days between 10 March and the end of June the cryptanalysts solved all the Shark signals.

In April, forewarned of U-boat positions and activities by Ultra, Allied navies took the offensive. Convoy escorts were strengthened. Warships were fitted with improved radar and high-frequency direction finding. New escort carriers joined the hunt. The number of ships sunk in convoy dropped by two-thirds, and the toll of U-boats climbed. That month U-boats sank 245,000 tons of shipping for the loss of fifteen U-boats.

Early in May a westbound convoy running empty from Britain was scattered by gales south-west of Greenland, and had the bad luck to meet up by chance with U-boat packs. Nine merchant ships were sunk for the loss of one U-boat. Soon afterwards Ultra provided the approximate locations of the U-boats involved and another nine were sunk. That same month two convoys crossed the Atlantic without loss while six U-boats were sunk. Shipping losses for that month were down to 165,000 tons and altogether 40 U-boats were sunk out of the 118 still in the Atlantic.

By this time, six months after the *Petard*'s capture of the Triton material, U-boat messages were being read almost every day, save for an occasional failure to find the day's entry code. One of these interruptions in the flow of Ultra came on 20 April after Ultra had warned that U-boat packs were lying in wait for a major convoy from Halifax. Fortunately the right cribs were found and after an agonising day of silence Ultra was quickly restored. The convoy of fifty-seven merchant ships, escorted by five warships, reached Britain from Halifax without loss, diverted around the U-boat packs on the basis of the Ultra intelligence. These fifty-seven ships unloaded badly needed cargoes after worrying months during which stocks were running down. They carried materials for the coming Normandy invasion and for British war factories: three of them carried grain and tanks, two carried steel and lumber, nine carried explosives, others were laden with fuel oil, lubricating oil, sugar, phosphates and general cargo.

The price in U-boat losses had become too high even for the tough commander of a service that reckoned to suffer heavy casualties, and in the last week of May Doenitz ordered his U-boats to leave the Atlantic shipping lanes and rest up in areas west of the Azores. It had taken just five weeks to turn the tide of the Battle of the Atlantic, a naval victory as great as any in the Royal Navy's history. Doenitz, still confident in the security of his Enigma signals, put his defeat down to improved Allied radar. During the following three summer months more U-boats than Allied merchant ships were sunk – seventy-four against fifty-eight.

Ralph Erskine, an authority on signals intelligence, told the author that continuity was extremely important in breaking any Enigma message, and using the materials captured by the *Petard* may have eased the way for Bletchley Park to break back into Shark when the Germans introduced a new rotor and reflector in July 1943.

Despite the German decision not to replace the sunk surface depot ships, U-boats were again able to spend long spells in the Atlantic because of 'milch cow' U-boats servicing them in remote parts of the ocean.

The positions of these had been known through Ultra, but the Admiralty, always worried that the Germans might realise that the Enigma was broken and use a new code, vetoed attacks on them until mid-1943, when their locations could be explained by air reconnaissance and improved radar. The Americans, who had long been pressing for these milch cows to be destroyed, finally persuaded the Admiralty that risks to Ultra were minimal. Between June and August US carrier planes sank five milch cow U-boats and reserve tankers.

From August 1943 naval Enigma was read regularly and rapidly without significant interruption for the rest of the war, and Churchill brought standing cheers in the House of Commons on 21 September when he announced that not one Allied merchant ship had been sunk in the North Atlantic in the previous three months. This situation had been brought about by a combination of factors, enabling Ultra intelligence – providing verbatim readings of signals between U-boat captains at sea and U-boat Command ashore – to be fully utilised.

British boffins (the wartime term for backroom scientists) had developed a new form of short-wave radar undetectable by U-boats, and U-boats cruising on the surface were often taken by surprise and subjected to sudden bombing attacks from unseen aircraft. Twenty-six U-boats were sunk and seventeen severely damaged between May and July. Doenitz accepted that these developments made the North Atlantic untenable for his U-boats.

Another factor was that the Portuguese agreed, after years of British pressure, to allow the establishment of Allied air bases in the Azores, finally closing the air-cover gap. Other factors were high-frequency direction-finding, and the production in British shipyards of fast escorts, River class frigates, able to cross the Atlantic without refuelling, speedy enough to outpace a surface U-boat which earlier ones were unable to do. The Allies had also developed escort carriers (called Woolworth Carriers) by putting flight decks on hulls built as merchant ships, and the mid-Atlantic air-cover gap was also being closed by land-based aircraft with longer range. Shipping needs were being met rapidly in American shipyards with prefabricated all-welded standardised merchant vessels – the famous 'Liberty' ships. They were built in around ten days and American shipyards were launching three a week.

In September Doenitz sent twenty-eight U-boats, fitted with enhanced anti-aircraft weapons, radar detectors and decoys, to renew attempts to cut the Atlantic lifeline, a struggle virtually abandoned since May. They also carried new *Zaunkönig* torpedoes equipped to home in on the pitch of the propellors of escort ships, which involved U-boats having to dive immediately after firing to avoid being chased by it themselves.

They no longer knew of the convoy arrangements because a new British convoy code was at last being used, and they had to cruise around on the chance of sighting Allied ships in the vastness of the ocean. A Canadian Liberator spotted and sank one on 19 September in the path of two convoys, and these were then combined in one convoy of sixty-six ships with fifteen warship escorts. This last convoy battle began the next day when HMS *Lagan* sank after its stern was blasted away, and in a running battle three warships and three merchant ships were sunk for the loss of three U-boats – two by aircraft and one by the destroyer *Keppel*.

RAF Coastal Command went on the offensive during this period with new centimetric radar and searchlights and took a heavy toll of returning U-boats, guided mostly by Ultra's charting of U-boat courses. The commander-in-chief, MRAF Sir John Slessor, wrote in a foreword to F.W. Winterbotham's book *The Ultra Secret*, published in 1974, 'I have the best reason to know that in the Battle of the Atlantic Ultra, in conjunction with HF/DF (Radar direction finding), was a real war winner.'

Later, the U-boats sailed, submerged, from their French bases into Spanish waters where they were able to surface and recharge their batteries. In October 1943, the Admiralty advised the Americans of Ultra information about refuelling due to take place north of the Azores, and American carrier planes found four U-boats on the surface and also sank the milch cow *U-460*. By November only one of ten milch cows in service in March was left. This brought a drastic cut in the number of U-boats operating in the Atlantic.

As U-boats returned to their bases they were fitted with new weapons, including acoustic torpedoes and a new apparatus called the schnorkel, a valved tube to the surface that enabled a U-boat to run underwater on its diesels, increasing its speed and range.

Meanwhile, Germany's heavy ships continued to be a great worry to British naval chiefs. In March Churchill had told the Russians that arctic convoys carrying supplies vital to the battle on the Russian front were taking unacceptable losses and had to be suspended. They were renewed in the autumn and three convoys got through to Murmansk without incident. As the third convoy returned empty it was spotted by a German reconnaissance plane. Adm Doenitz, under Hitler's threat of scrapping his major surface ships, decided to risk the battleship *Scharnhorst* in an effort to destroy the next convoy. He called it Operation Eastern Front because the convoy was thought likely to be carrying 400 aircraft and 4,000 tanks, and destroying them would be of vast help to the German forces retreating after Russia's victory at Kursk.

Scharnhorst was the only heavy ship available, as the newest and most powerful German ship, the *Tirpitz*, was under repair after attacks by midget submarines and heavy RAF bombing. Ultra intelligence advised Adm Sir Bruce Fraser, the Commander-in-Chief, Home Fleet, that the *Scharnhorst* had sailed with an escort of five destroyers on Christmas Day afternoon, heading for the vital convoy. Adm Fraser sailed in his flagship, the battleship *Duke of York*, to join the convoy's strong escort force of cruisers and destroyers. The *Scharnhorst*'s destroyers were searching for the convoy when the British cruisers *Belfast*, *Sheffield*, and *Norfolk* came upon the *Scharnhorst* sailing unescorted. Exchanges of fire damaged the *Norfolk* and *Sheffield* but the *Scharnhorst* showed no sign of the hits claimed by all three cruisers and she headed south at 30 knots, only to run into the *Duke of York*, supported by the cruiser *Jamaica*.

Surprised, the *Scharnhorst* turned back north as ¾-ton shells from an accurate broadside crashed into her, visibly slowing her down. Two of the *Scharnhorst*'s 11-in shells passed through the *Duke of York*'s hollow masts without exploding. In a 90-minute duel the pride of the German Navy was battered to pieces after torpedoes from destroyers reduced her speed to 5 knots. In all, fifty-five torpedoes were aimed at her before she finally sank. Only 36 of her 2,000 crew were picked out of the freezing sea. This important British victory is known as the Battle of North Cape.

Ultra reported that the protective torpedo nets around the *Tirpitz* – her latest repairs completed – were to be lifted from 1 April 1944, and she would be undergoing sea trials outside Altenfjord in Norway. She was attacked by forty-four bombers from the carriers *Victorious* and *Furious*. Only secondary damage was done to the heavily armoured hull, but she was out of action for another three months. That meant not a single German capital ship was ready to oppose the Allied invasion armada in June. *Tirpitz* was finally finished off when the RAF hit her with a 21-ft long Tallboy bomb in Altenfjord in August.

By this time patrolling aircraft were taking a large toll of U-boats, sinking twenty-three in the six weeks before Doenitz ordered another withdrawal from the Atlantic. Ten convoys crossed the ocean between mid-December and mid-January without any sign of U-boats. At the end of January 1944 Doenitz made another attempt with twenty-two U-boats in waters west of Ireland swarming with Allied convoys. They sank only one merchant ship and the sloop HMS *Woodpecker* and shot down two Coastal Command planes. Eleven U-boats were sunk, six of them by depth charges from Capt Johnnie Walker's five-sloop escort group. Doenitz sent most of the U-boats that survived that battle back into the same area at the end of February in a wolf-pack of sixteen. By 22 March, when Doenitz recalled the survivors, they had sunk a sloop and a corvette for the loss of seven U-boats.

In the first three months of 1944 U-boats sank only 3 of the 3,360 merchant ships escorted in vast convoys across the Atlantic, while 36 U-boats were sunk. By the end of 1944, the last full year of the war, 241 U-boats failed to return to their bases. During the first half of 1944 most of the U-boats were concentrated around coastal waters of the British Isles to harry the build-up of forces in Britain for the expected Allied invasion of the continent. They sank two British frigates and an American landing ship while submerged, and one hit four American supply ships off Selsey Bill near Portsmouth. All U-boats escaped.

Ultra contributed immensely to preventing serious intervention by the German Navy against the vast armada of Allied ships that carried invasion forces across the Channel for the 6 June D-Day landings, and subsequently. Since the threat of heavy warships and the Luftwaffe no longer existed, the most serious threat to invasion shipping was seen by Allied chiefs as coming from some 500 U-boats at ports in the Bay of Biscay. Because of the breakdown of land communications as a result of Allied bombing Adm Doenitz had to rely on radio for communications with his U-boat commanders, and Bletchley Park was reading most of his orders. In the middle of May 1944, Bletchley Park read a signal from U-boat Command to the admiral commanding western France, disclosing that forty U-boats would sail against the invasion fleet on D-Day or D+1. It also gave the areas for other standing U-boat patrols – off the Scilly Isles, towards north Cornwall and a reserve position in the Bay of Biscay. To ensure that the best use was made of the continuous flow of Ultra intelligence from Bletchley Park the head of the Submarine Tracking Room transferred his U-boat plotting to Plymouth.

When D-Day came the U-boats were taken by

surprise by Allied disinformation ruses, and the German High Command informed the U-boats in the early hours of that morning that the invasion was taking place in Seine Bay. In all thirty-five U-boats left port late on 6 June, six of them fitted with schnorkels, and headed into the Channel, nine others operated off the coasts of Devon and Cornwall, the rest formed a defensive line off the French west coast and were joined by eight more diverted from Atlantic operations. They had little success against the weight of Allied anti-U-boat forces. In three months eighteen ships supplying the invasion forces were sunk, for the loss of thirty-five U-boats. In August Doenitz withdrew the remainder. The fitting of schnorkels at the Biscay U-boat bases had continued after the Normandy landings, but as Allied forces approached, the U-boats departed from one base after another. All were transferred to Norway, from where they concentrated operations in British coastal waters; the development of the schnorkel allowed them to operate unseen and gave them the ability of fast escape once detected.

In September *U-482* sank a corvette and four cargo ships off Northern Ireland en route to Liverpool, having travelled 2,500 miles of its 2,730-mile voyage submerged. Only two U-boats were sunk that month, mainly because there were fewer operational.

Ultra reported in October that six U-boats in ports in southern Norway were being prepared for cruises of eleven weeks' duration, indicating an intention to go around the British Isles and into the Channel. Doenitz exhorted his crews: 'Resumption of U-boat warfare must and will be Germany's main aim . . . it may be found that, after all, the final issue of the war will be decided by the new campaign that is now gathering way with initial prospects that are wholly favourable. Before the end of the present year decisive effects must be achieved.'

Anti-submarine forces that had been switched from the English Channel to the area of north-east Scotland were brought back to the Channel to meet this threat. There was a brief flare-up in activity close to the Cherbourg peninsula around Christmas when six ships were sunk in six days, mainly by one U-boat. The last German counter-offensive in the Ardennes, which relied on bad weather to ground superior Allied air power, was planned on the basis of weather reports sent from U-boats in the North Atlantic.

The U-boat effort in the English Channel was completely defeated. Of the enormous mass of invasion shipping they sank 33 merchant ships and 9 warships. At least 46 U-boats were destroyed in the same area. During the last four months of 1944 12,000 Allied ships crossed the Atlantic safely. U-boats sank 4 ships in British waters and 2 in the Atlantic. At the beginning of 1945 naval chiefs were again deeply worried about a new U-boat threat. Their concern was based on the elusiveness the U-boats gained with the schnorkel and intelligence about a new type of electro-U-boat, prefabricated in eight sections at dispersed factories, and already undergoing sea trials in the Baltic. They had learned of this threat from American interception of technical messages sent by the Japanese naval attaché in Berlin to Tokyo.

The RAF were called upon to fulfil the earlier promise of Bomber Harris, and at this late stage in the war Bomber Command became the main instrument of U-boat destruction. They carried out heavy raids on factories and yards making the components, the ports where they were being assembled, and the routes used to transport the sections, principally the Dortmund–Ems canal from the Ruhr to the North Sea.

Production of U-boats fell off for the first time, mainly because of Allied armies overrunning the U-boat shipyards in Germany. Until then U-boat output had been steadily increasing despite air attacks, and 120 of the super-fast electro-U-boats were completed.

On 25 February a smaller coastal electro-boat, *U-2322*, sank the small British freighter, SS *Egholm* (1,317 tons), off the east coast of Scotland. British warships began an immediate chase but the U-boat escaped unscathed, and its pursuers were amazed at its underwater speed which made their depth-charge attacks seem pointless.

At a meeting with Hitler, Doenitz told him that he hoped to get enough of these new craft together to cut supplies to the Allied forces, and then return to attack the convoy route again. He explained, 'A complete transformation of the war at sea has been brought to fruition by this complete underwater vessel. The deadly weapon of the pure U-boat is at hand.' Had the war in Europe continued for a further two years – as had seemed likely before Bletchley Park's use of the material captured by HMS *Petard* to provide the Ultra intelligence that led to victory in the critical 1943 phase of the U-boat war – Doenitz would have gained another chance with terrible consequences for Britain. He could also have carried the war to the American homeland.

But the weight of RAF bombing intensified, and this plan had come too late. Instead, Doenitz had a last fling in the Atlantic. In April six U-boats with schnorkel were on course for the United States. The Americans, warned by Ultra and fearing the U-boats might be fitted with the V2 rockets used against England, sent twenty destroyers to hunt them. Three U-boats were sunk in early contacts, and another was sunk shortly after it sank the destroyer *Frederick T. Davis*. The other two were not found, but they gave themselves up after Germany surrendered.

The first large electro-U-boat (type XXI) left Bergen on 30 April bound for the Caribbean. A second sailed from Wilhelmshaven on the German North Sea on 3 May as the British Army were on the outskirts of the navy base. They were among the forty-nine U-boats at sea when Doenitz, appointed to succeed as German leader after Hitler's suicide, ordered them to surface and surrender at the nearest Allied port. Until then, they had been a constant threat, tying down huge Allied resources.

In the last five months of the war 153 U-boats were sunk, the last one – the *U-320* – on 7 May when it was bombed and sunk by a Catalina of RAF Coastal Command between the Shetlands and Norway. That same day two merchant ships and a Norwegian minesweeper were torpedoed and sunk by U-boats which had not heard the surrender order because they had been submerged for several days.

The crews of U-boats suffered a heavy toll. Of nearly 40,900 men who served in U-boats during the war, 25,800 were lost at sea and 5,000 captured, a loss rate of 76 per cent. German shipyards built 1,162 U-boats; 842 sailed on operations and 784 (93 per cent) were lost, 696 by enemy action; 220 were scuttled rather than surrender, 156 surrendered, 2 fled to Argentina and the remainder were in bases in Norway and Germany.

The highest scoring U-boat of the war was *U-48*. Between September 1939 and June 1941 she sank fifty-one ships totalling 310,407 tons. Over 200,000 depth charges were dropped, one in sixteen attacks were successful. Depth charges from British warships sank 158 U-boats (see Appendix Two – destroyer losses).

When the Battle of the Atlantic ended 2,452 Allied ships (totalling 12.8 million tons) had been sunk in the North Atlantic. The global total of merchant ships lost was 5,150 (21,570,720 tons). The British Merchant Navy lost 30,248 men and the Royal Navy 73,642, mostly in the Atlantic, where U-boats sank 175 warships, mostly British. RAF Coastal Command lost 5,866 men and 1,777 aircraft. The Royal Canadian Navy lost 1,965 men.

Because of these losses and the virtual collapse of its export trade, and with housing and industry wrecked by years of bombing, victorious Britain faced the postwar years as the world's largest debtor nation. Adm Doenitz, still blithely unaware of the breaking of his Enigma signals, wrote in his 1958 memoirs, 'Radar and particularly radar location by aircraft, had to all practical purposes robbed the U-boats of their power to fight on the surface. Wolf-pack operations against convoys in the North Atlantic, the main theatre of operations, were no longer possible. They could only be resumed if we succeeded in radically increasing the fighting power of the U-boats. I accordingly withdrew them from the North Atlantic. On May 24 (1943) I ordered them to proceed, using the utmost caution, to the area south-west of the Azores. We had lost the Battle of the Atlantic.'

On VE day HMS *Petard* – early in its second commission, with a new crew of mainly 'hostilities only' youngsters still at school when war began – was in dry dock at Wallsend-on-Tyne, having sprung leaks from her own depth charges during attacks on a U-boat picked up by Asdic off the north-east of Scotland. She had made a pattern of attacks, but clearly the schnorkel enabled the U-boat to escape. Shortly afterwards she sailed from Gourock down the Clyde, bound for the continuing war against the Japanese. From her deck the author saw several U-boats berthed side by side, having obeyed calls to surrender. The crews of several surrendered U-boats watched her curiously, little knowing, as neither did the *Petard*'s own fresh young crew, the huge contribution she had made to their defeat. For this was to remain, perhaps, the war's biggest secret for decades afterwards.

Part Two
HMS Petard *Fights On*

Chapter Six

Victory and Defeat in the Mediterranean

While renewed Ultra U-boat intelligence was turning the tide in the Atlantic Battle, HMS *Petard* was heavily engaged in the eastern Mediterranean, where the Army and the RAF were also fighting desperate battles. Her crew, totally unaware of their developing contribution to winning the Atlantic battle, returned from relaxation in the Holy Land to find they had a new first lieutenant, Lt David Dunbar-Nasmith RN, son of a First World War admiral famed for winning the Victoria Cross, already mentioned in dispatches.

Five days later *Petard* was in action again while escorting supply ships into the newly recaptured Egyptian port of Mersa Matruh. Her gunners, forewarned of approaching bombers by RDF, opened up as they came within range, and fifty bombs fell around the four ships. Four days later *Petard* joined four cruisers and twenty-two destroyers escorting four merchant ships carrying aviation fuel, ammunition and other stores to beleaguered Malta. The convoy was attacked repeatedly, but Italian and German planes were warded off by heavy anti-aircraft fire, though near misses caused splinter damage. In a dusk assault at wave-top height, six Ju 88 torpedo bombers failed to make a hit. Just after dark the following day the convoy was lit up by flares and twenty-six Ju 88 torpedo bombers came in from all directions. One torpedo hit the bows of the cruiser *Arethusa*, killing 157, wounding many others and causing severe damage. *Petard* towed her back to Alexandria and fended off several attacks by formations of Ju 88 bombers. Meanwhile, the convoy got through to Malta without losing a ship, the first to reach the besieged island in nearly two years.

A fortnight later, on 30 November, *Petard* joined an escort of four cruisers and twenty destroyers for another convoy to Malta, this time guarding a petrol tanker and three other merchant ships. At dusk the next day a number of Ju 88 torpedo bombers were forced by the heavy barrage of twenty-four warships to launch their torpedoes at long range so that all ships had time to take evasive action and not one was hit. More bombing and torpedo attacks followed but none was pressed home, and the convoy reached Malta without loss. Amid all this *Petard* picked up the crew of a Wellington bomber shot down the day before. She was at the rear of the convoy and ships ahead of her had failed to see the dinghy. *Petard*'s sharp lookouts spotted a small torch, all that the men in the dinghy had left to signal with, having used up all their flares without being seen. Thousands of Maltese, suffering food shortages as well as heavy bombing, lined the Grand Harbour to welcome them with rousing cheers.

Petard escorted nine empty cargo vessels back to Port Said, but although bombed every day, no ships were lost and *Petard*'s gunners shot down a Ju 88, the ship's first aircraft kill. Reg Crang noted:

Great cheers went up as the Ju 88, having dropped its torpedo, strayed too close and got a bellyful of bullets. As it banked into a turn our pom-poms and Oerlikons poured fire into it from less than 500 feet. The bomber plunged into the sea quite near us, turning over as it hit the water. However, next morning it seemed we had been singled out for revenge. Three times German bombers screamed in close straddling the *Petard* with a stick of bombs. One exploded so close to the side that the ship was drenched in spray and bucked like a bronco. Lights went out and anything loose jumped all over the place. Fortunately we had a bit of air cover and we saw our fighters shoot down two German planes.

Petard's gunners shot down their second Ju 88 a few days later while escorting a convoy to Tobruk.

The Navy's main task at this time was to protect merchant ships carrying supplies to Libyan ports as the Eighth Army advanced and to prevent the escape of Axis forces from North Africa. The C-in-C sent a general signal to all British warships, ordering them to 'Sink, burn and destroy. Let nothing pass.' *Petard* searched two hospital ships without finding fit troops aboard them.

On 13 December – the day the first Enigma Triton messages were being read at Bletchley Park – *Petard* sailed from Tobruk to Benghazi, entering the harbour there as a heavy air raid began. Reg Crang noted, 'It was like going into an inferno with bombs crashing into the harbour and all our guns firing blindly as we pushed in to find a berth. A nearby tanker was hit and burning oil spilt out and spread over the water setting fire to smaller wooden ships. As we tied up the RASC came to collect their stores, shrugging off the bombardment going on all around them.'

Sailing with *Queen Olga* for Malta next day they had been warned that a British submarine, *P-35*, was operating along their course. Just after 3 a.m. next day, as a new watch came on duty, lookouts spotted a vessel 3,000 yd off the port bow heading on the same course. It was a dark, moonless night and it was thought to be a surface vessel. But as the destroyers approached, powerful night binoculars revealed it was a submarine, recharging its batteries. Thinking they had met with the *P-35* earlier than expected Lt Cdr Thornton acted with caution. He ordered the signalman to send a challenge on his lantern. The submarine, then abeam, responded by firing two torpedoes and crash-diving. The Asdic hut reported the torpedoes advancing and *Petard*'s helm was turned hard to port to take her between the phosphorescent tracks of the torpedoes.

Jack Hall was on duty in the Asdic hut and with a firm contact he passed ranges and bearings of the submarine's movements. There was no wind and the sea was smooth. *Petard* dropped one depth charge fused to explode at 50 ft, followed by pattern depth-charge attacks by both ships, damaging the submarine and forcing her to surface. Forewarned by the Asdic hut that the submarine was blowing its tanks, *Petard*'s 36-in searchlight was focused on the conning tower as it broke the surface only a cable's distance – 200 yards – off the *Petard*'s starboard beam. It was quickly crossed by *Queen Olga*'s searchlight.

Oerlikon gunner John Mackness told the author what happened next. He said, 'The captain yelled "Open fire" and I riddled the conning tower and fired into figures running along the casing towards the deck gun. The captain had given a standing order that firing was to be kept up so that the crew would stay in the submarine and not scuttle it.' The submarine was also swept with pom-pom shells. (It was later known that the enemy was the Italian submarine *Uarsciek* on her twenty-fifth patrol. Her captain had ordered all the crew to abandon ship immediately she surfaced, and he was among the first to be killed as others dived overboard or took shelter.)

Lt Cdr Thornton's report, classified 'Most Secret' by the Admiralty until released to the Public Record Office in 1977, related the start of the action and then continued, 'Up till this time the ship had carried out the unpleasant duty of raking the U-boat with small arms fire as the crew were abandoning ship, thus massacring a number of them. An able seaman called out to a man on her casing to go below and shut off her engines. Luckily for the Italian I did not see him or he would have been shot. As it was he stopped the engines even though he was suffering from severe splinter wounds. I went alongside with the intention of stripping her before she sank. Instead a tow rope was fixed and a prize crew was left on board. Queen Olga was ordered to stop picking up survivors and screen.'

Others watching from the *Petard* recalled the killing of the Italian submariners differently. They saw men, some naked, slithering down from the conning tower onto the submarine casing being blown apart by pom-pom shells and oerlikon fire. Reg Crang noted:

As naked men emerged from the conning tower to drop on to the casing both warships opened up a murderous fusillade of fire. No-one on the deck could escape the slaughter. After a long pause with no more firing the Petard moved in closer. A few more naked men came out, we thought to surrender, but a machine gun on the bridge opened up and began to pick them off. Our crew were aghast at what we thought to be the captain's own act of vengeance. Mercifully it soon stopped but by now the Petard was so close to the submarine that it could not avoid collision. With a sickening crunch the Petard half rammed, half climbed onto the hull of the submarine. Then, with engines astern, it backed off. Thought could now be given to rescuing the survivors instead of killing them. Daylight was breaking and the Italian sailors started jumping into the sea and swimming towards us. Many were crying out what sounded to me like 'Aiota', presumably 'Help'. A few, possibly injured or perhaps non-swimmers, drifted away out of reach and beyond help. It was pitiful to see.

A few hours later the Italian submarine began to sink, and the prize crew returned to the *Petard* as it slid beneath the waves. Reg Crang wrote in his diary:

We were very disappointed to miss out on the honour of bringing back such a sensational prize. We reached Malta in late afternoon. Word had somehow got around and a large crowd had gathered. When the skipper ordered the Italian flag to be waved they broke into loud cheers. But many of us did not feel like gloating over our success. I do not think I shall ever forget the cry of 'Aiota' from drowning men.

In his book written two decades later Gordon Connell, a sub-lieutenant at the time, recalled:

Ceasefire bells were ringing, stilling the murderous chatter of close range weapons, and many stood appalled and numbed by what we saw in obscene searchlights. For a while there was a pause, then more white figures, most naked, appeared out of the conning tower, cringed in the terrible blinding beams, stumbled through the awful bloody debris of their comrades. The voice of the captain could be heard in the still air calling for fire to be re-opened. The guns remained silent, they could not be depressed sufficiently to hit the submarine, men also hesitated to obey, everyone overwhelmed by the slaughter. Seconds ticked away, more figures tumbled out of the conning tower and the captain repeated his order.

From the dark of the open bridge a Lewis gun began its ghastly solo, directed at men running aft. Bullets tore into the bodies below, three or four fell before the firing stopped abruptly, the captain trying frantically to avoid collision. He had failed to see that the submarine was on a collision course. The ship hit Uarsciek's pressure hull with a crunch, half riding over the submarine before sliding back clear under emergency full astern.

It was not until the cries of wounded and drowning men, heard at the moment of impact, confirmed the submarine's nationality that Mark Thornton's terrible doubt that it could have been the British *P-35* was resolved. The first round of gunfire had done what was intended, it put the submarine's gun out of action and killed the Italian captain in the act of ditching his confidential books. They were found by his body weighted in a sack.

Petard's second salvo of slaughter was probably justified, the men running aft towards the dome may have set out on a suicide bid to activate an anti-capture or self-destructive device, unlikely but possible. In war it was not possible to take chances, but the counter action was still horrifying.

The former oerlikon gunner, John Mackness, told the author, 'I felt very bad about it. I must have hit quite a lot of them. But in wartime it was a question of killing the enemy before he could have a go at you.'

Mervyn Romeril, now a retired Bournemouth bank manager, saw it all. He told the author, 'I was the loader for the starboard oerlikon and remember very vividly the moment we were ordered to open fire on the Italian crew. It was like a shooting gallery at a fair ground. I saw men blown into the air before falling in the water. They had been trying to man the gun on the U-boat casing, and it was a case of them or us. That's war. It was a horrifying scene, and it's haunted me for years.' Asked whether he recalled a machine-gun being fired from the bridge after the ceasefire bell had been rung, he said, 'I don't recall a Lewis gun, or any firing after the cease-fire. At one time we had an Italian rapid firing gun somebody had picked up in Mersa Matruh or Tobruk, mounted on the guard rails near the torpedo tubes.'

Ted Saunders recalled, 'One of the Italians taken aboard had his arm shredded. We had only local anaesthetic, so the doctor gave him rum, amputated his arm and ordered what was left of it to be thrown overboard.' What about the firing of a Lewis gun? 'Yes there was a Lewis gun aboard, firing .303 bullets. I wouldn't be at all surprised if the skipper was firing it from the bridge.'

Thirty-two prisoners were taken aboard the *Petard*. The wounded, several seriously so, were treated by

Surgeon-Lt William Prendergast, a volunteer from County Derry, who was heard loudly condemning the bloodshed.

Lt Cdr Thornton DSO, RN, was awarded the Distinguished Service Cross and the Admiralty diplomatically waived its rule against a joint award for the same action by permitting him to accept the Greek Military Cross. The recommendation stated, 'Petard was particularly well handled throughout and nearly successful in bringing the surrendered submarine to port. Her boarding party was led with dash and determination.'

Lt David Arthur Dunbar-Nasmith RN was awarded the DSC, and Yeoman of Signals Randell Chapman and LS Trevor Tipping received Distinguished Service Medals. Midshipman Peter Thomas Alleyne Goddard RN who commanded the prize crew, and Signalman Kenneth Hannay were mentioned in despatches.

For three weeks over Christmas and the New Year *Petard* was twice in dry dock at Alexandria for repairs to her bows resulting from the collision with the Italian submarine. During this time Lt Cdr Thornton left the ship. Surgeon-Lt Prendergast had reported that his captain needed a medical check, and his replacement quickly followed. Lt Cdr Rupert Egan took command when *Petard* left dry dock at the end of January.

Early in April 1943, *Petard* and *Paladin* made a night dash at top speeds of 36 knots to bombard the Tunisian port of Sousse a few miles ahead of the Eighth Army's advance. Using charts captured from the Italian submarine *Uarsciek* they passed safely through minefields, narrowly escaping detection by patrolling German U-boats and appeared off Sousse, where they could see the flashing of Eighth Army guns in the desert beyond.

They ranged their 4-in guns on a flashing blue light at the end of the harbour mole, apparently left on to guide in an expected supply convoy. Both ships fired eight salvoes, then reversing course they fired another six salvoes before the blue light went out. As they headed away a line of E-boats straddled their course. *Paladin*, closely followed by *Petard* in line astern, headed straight at the E-boats, both ships opening fire with oerlikons and pom-pom guns while making screening smoke. The E-boats raked both ships with machine-gun fire, but nobody was hit and only minor damage was done.

During the next six weeks *Petard* escorted supply ships to Tripoli and newly captured Sfax, sailing through areas of sea dotted with floating mines. The deck crew was kept busy exploding them with rifle fire. At dusk on 24 April, unsighted by lookouts or detected by radar, enemy planes dived out of the gloom and raked the *Petard* from the stern to the bridge with cannon and machine-gun fire. The whole of Y gun's crew were wiped out, three killed instantly and the gun captain critically wounded. One member of the ammunition party was also killed and ten wounded, four very seriously. It was thought to have been one plane that had passed so fast that nobody could identify its type, but oerlikon gunner John Mackness, just 5 ft 3 in, recalls seeing four Ju 88s in line astern. He said, 'If I'd been six inches taller I'd have had my head blown off. There were bullet holes in the ammunition locker behind me.'

Mervyn Romeril was on duty as bridge lookout, having been moved just that day from passing ammunition to Y gun, a move that may have saved his life. He recalled, 'I was only aware of one plane attacking, but I ducked down on seeing tracer bullets overhead.'

Off Malta, after a night at action stations, lookouts shouted that a submarine had surfaced a little to starboard just ahead of the *Petard*. Pom-poms opened fire on the conning tower and the submarine fired a torpedo and crash-dived. The *Petard* heeled over to port as she turned hard to avoid the track of the torpedo which passed close to the starboard quarter. Then to the crew's surprise the *Petard* continued on her way at full speed. Reg Crang noted, 'The skipper, so dependable, had just enough time to avoid the torpedo. But it was a close call. It seemed a clear case to follow up with a depth charge attack but we steamed on, evidently because it might have been a British submarine!'

Twenty miles off Cape Bon on the night of 4 May, *Petard*, *Paladin* and *Nubian* sank the Italian destroyer *Campobasso* and the large merchant ship *Perseo*, carrying motor transport, bombs and land mines. The cargo went up in a huge explosion within sight of the enemy's last redoubt in North Africa where the *Perseo*'s supplies were desperately needed.

With Rommel's surrender in Tunisia on 12 May, the Allied air forces and the Navy turned its heavy firepower on the Italian island of Pantellaria in the Sicilian Channel, dominating the narrow stretch of sea linking the eastern and western sides of the Mediterranean. The *Petard* was involved from the start of operations, code-named Retribution, and on the day the North African campaign ended, she joined the *Isis* and *Nubian* as escorts to the cruiser *Orion* at the start of the Sicily campaign. They sailed inshore within sight of the 11-in coastal batteries, which quickly found their

range, for their first two salvoes straddled the *Petard*.
As she headed seawards after laying smoke to screen
the big ships, shells fell so close to her stern that they
buckled the plates and let in water. Pumps dealt with it
all the way back to Malta.

At the beginning of July hopes of home leave were
raised when *Petard* sailed past Gibraltar into the
Atlantic, but this prospect was quickly dispelled. She
joined fifteen other destroyers in a force that included
the battleships *Howe*, *King George V*, *Nelson*, *Rodney*,
Warspite and *Valiant*, and aircraft carriers *Indomitable*
and *Formidable*, on the way to cover the invasion of
Sicily.

The landings began on 10 July while the naval forces
patrolled well out to sea from the landing beaches to
make sure the Italian Navy could not intervene. After
the first day the *Petard* was detached and ordered to
Malta for a special task.

At 2 a.m. on 12 July Gen Dwight Eisenhower, the
Allied Supreme Commander, embarked with his staff
officers, and *Petard* took them to the British beach at
Pachino, where an assault launch came alongside and
took Eisenhower and his party to the headquarters ship
Largs for a conference with Gen Bernard Montgomery.
On his return an hour later *Petard* dashed at 34 knots
to Porto Palo Bay on the eastern side of Cape Passaro
where Eisenhower talked with Lt Gen Miles Dempsey
and the Naval Force Commander, Rear Adm Sir Philip
Vian. There was no sign of fighting at either beach,
the advance having already moved inland. At noon
Eisenhower returned to *Petard* and was taken back to
Malta. Reg Crang noted, 'When one young matelot
dared to ask for his autograph he obliged with a "Sure
lad" remark. Other lads followed suit. When Jimmy

(the First Lieutenant) found out what was going on he nearly shaved off and stamped on it straight away. On our way round the coast an enemy gun fired three rounds at us. All shots fell well short so there was no danger, but it made the general jump. We felt honoured to have been entrusted with this assignment.'

Next day, while bombarding traffic on a coast road near Catania, East Sicily, *Petard* was hit by fire from a tank. The shell went right through the ship, drilling a neat hole as it went, but causing no other damage. That same evening *Petard* was among four destroyers bombarding a Catania airfield when her RDF picked up a Ju 88 coming in low from astern, and the operator shouted a warning down the bridge voice pipe. *Petard* was swung hard to starboard, and a torpedo ran along the port side, a near miss. Reg Crang elatedly recorded, 'This is the clearest case so far of the RDF proving its worth and our morale has gone up considerably.'

During that week *Petard* took part in two daylight bombardments of Catania, part of the destroyer screen close inshore, with 15-in shells from the battleship *Warspite*, a veteran of Jutland, passing over them. Malta was heavily bombed the night *Petard* returned, but she escaped damage. The following day, with five other destroyers, she escorted the cruisers *Aurora* and *Penelope* for a night bombardment of Cotrone on the heel of mainland Italy. *Petard* fired 160 4-in shells.

On 30 July *Petard* was damaged while going alongside the battleship *Warspite* to exchange documents at a speed of 20 knots. It caused dents and gashes and flooding in one magazine, and to the crew's delight the *Petard* returned to Malta for repairs. Reg Crang wrote, 'We reckon we deserved a break, this week we have been at sea most days carrying out anti-submarine patrols, escorting some LSTs to Syracuse and even on fleet exercises.'

Back at sea on 6 August *Petard* and *Queen Olga* towed landing craft to beaches behind the enemy lines on the east coast of Sicily. The soldiers were carried aboard the destroyers before transferring to the landing craft for a night landing to blow up bridges and disrupt the enemy retreat. They were left to make their own way to Allied lines. Then the *Petard* was engaged in early morning bombardments along the Calabrian coast. This severely disrupted enemy lorry and railway transport. Engine drivers sought shelter by stopping in tunnels, leaving a tail of wagons in the open as sitting targets. Reg Crang noted, 'We went in so close there was danger of grounding. We caused havoc to both road convoys and freight trains, targets unmissable from short range. An ammunition train blew up with a tremendous explosion, and goods wagons were seen tumbling down from the clifftop railway to the beach. Several times we encountered retaliatory fire from artillery and tanks. They ought to have hit us because now and then we were straddled with shells.'

While briefly based in Augusta, where the crew particularly enjoyed grapes and tomatoes, having had no fresh vegetables for many weeks, the *Petard* carried out offensive patrols in the Strait of Messina, her guns putting out a searchlight one night, and also escorted the battleships *Rodney* and *Nelson* during heavy bombardments.

By the middle of August the Allies occupied the whole of Sicily, and Montgomery's Eighth Army was poised to cross the narrow strip of sea to invade mainland Italy, where Mussolini had already been overthrown. A new government appointed by King Victor Emmanuel signed a secret armistice on 3 September. That same day, the fourth anniversary of the war, the Eighth Army moved across the Strait of Messina to land unopposed on the toe of Italy.

Six days later the *Petard* was one of twelve destroyers escorting a convoy, headed by two battleships and an aircraft carrier, to Taranto, where they landed 6,000 men of the 1st Airborne Division, carried in the warships because no aircraft were available. The fleet came under heavy air attack during passage through the Ionian Sea but the ship's ack-ack guns and air support from the carrier prevented any loss, though a cruiser was sunk by a mine.

Oerlikon gunner John Mackness recalled, 'The planes were coming in at such low level that shrapnel from our own 4-inch guns was coming down like hail.' The *Petard* picked up the four-man crews of two Ju 88 torpedo bombers shot down inside the destroyer screen while trying to get at the battleships. Reg Crang noted in his diary, 'I think we have now rescued seven boats of survivors (37 men in all including 28 Germans) a great tribute to our look-outs who are second to none in spotting small objects.'

The remaining ships of the Italian fleet in Taranto harbour were ordered to sail to Malta to surrender, and in savage Luftwaffe attacks the Italian Navy's flagship and newest battleship, the *Roma*, was sunk in a direct hit from a guided glider bomb.

While Taranto was being occupied Operation Avalanche, the largest amphibious operation of the war so far, began. The Allied Fifth Army, comprising the British 10th Corps and the US 6th Corps, were landed in the Gulf of Salerno south of Naples and in the Gulf of Policastro a little further south. Four bridgeheads were established against stubborn German resistance. Massive German reinforcements poured into Italy, took control of Rome, rescued Mussolini from a mountain-top prison, and drove on southwards to oppose the Allied beachheads.

With the surrender of the Italian Navy the major naval ships were ordered home, and the crew of the *Petard* were delighted to be among destroyers escorting them. Hopes were high that this time they really were on their way home, but soon after leaving Malta, bound for Gibraltar, the fleet was ordered to return. There was a crisis over a fierce German offensive by elements of five German panzer divisions against the Salerno beachhead, and the American 6th Corps were hanging on almost at the waters edge. The fleet's heavy guns were expected to break up the panzers, but plans were also being made for evacuation.

The *Petard* joined four other destroyers escorting the battleships *Warspite* and *Valiant* for bombardment of enemy concentrations in the hills behind the beaches. On the afternoon of 15 September *Petard*'s motor cutter landed the *Warspite*'s forward observation party on the beach and waited just offshore, while American soldiers lay in shallow trenches scooped out of the sand just above the high water mark. The destroyers laid a smokescreen to shield the heavy ships that lay only 2,000 yd offshore, and the forward observation team pinpointed targets. The *Warspite*'s eight 15-in guns thundered full broadsides, the huge shells whistling over the *Petard*, followed by bombardment from the British cruisers *Penelope*, *Aurora*, *Mauritius* and the USS *Philadelphia*, while British and US destroyers joined in.

Petard, close offshore, was firing her 4-in salvoes into the hillside just above the American forward positions.

Allied air forces added to the uproar by heavy bombing and strafing during pauses in the naval bombardment. The main target was the Sele valley, where on 14 September four German divisions supported by Tiger tanks had driven a two miles wide divide between the US bridgehead and the British 10th Corps, which had landed on their flank to the north.

The weight of explosives on troops, tanks and supplies smashed the German offensive, and the British 7th Armoured Division, carried in three cruisers from Tripoli, was put ashore. The Eighth Army linked up with the 5th Army beachhead on 16 September, and the Germans fell back to a fortified line across Italy south of Rome. The German War Diary revealed, 'Our attack had to stop . . . because of the great effect of the enemy sea bombardment and continuous air attacks.'

As daylight faded the two battleships threaded their way through the clusters of shipping off the beaches, which had suffered heavy losses from the radio-controlled glider bombs, and headed back to sea. They were followed by the Luftwaffe which concentrated heavy bombing and torpedo attacks on them. The heavy ack-ack guns of the battleships put up a huge barrage.

A shell hit the *Petard* as her guns were also blazing away. It blew a hole above the waterline 2–3 ft in diameter, and fragments caused casualties and damage. Two men were killed outright and were buried at sea shortly afterwards. Six others were wounded, three of them seriously. Reg Crang recorded, 'Our battleships were using secondary armament at low angle against wave-hopping torpedo bombers. A 6-inch shell, probably from the Warspite, exploded in the forward seamen's mess deck right amongst the ammunition supply part to A and B guns.' One of the wounded was

Asdic operator Jack Hall, whose action station when he was not on duty in the Asdic hut, was on a mess deck below A gun, from where he passed shells from the magazine hoist up a chute to A gun on the forecastle deck. He recalled it some fifty-five years later:

There was an explosion, a shower of sparks, then complete darkness. I stumbled towards the upper deck and didn't realise I'd been hit until I started blowing up my life-jacket and saw blood bubbling from a hole in my chest. I made my way to the sick bay where the MO treated my wound. Shrapnel had torn a groove across my back and another piece had gone through my back and come out at the front. Later I heard that my two shipmates had been blown to pieces and volunteers were asked for to collect their remains and put them in hammocks for burial. Nobody volunteered so two men were detailed and given a double tot of rum.

After a few uneventful Adriatic patrols *Petard* was ordered to Alexandria in company with the *Panther* to replace losses in the Aegean campaign. The Royal Navy suffered grievous losses in the disastrous Aegean campaign – an attempt to capitalise on the Italian surrender by seizing the Greek Dodecanese Islands, mainly occupied by Italian forces.

When Italy surrendered Hitler ordered swift measures to take over the Dodecanese from their Italian garrisons. The German Fliegerkorps, with hundreds of Ju 87s, Ju 88s, Me 110s and Me 109s, landed at the airfields in Rhodes, and German troops began moves onto other islands. Through a steady flow of intercepted German signals Churchill knew of these German moves but pressed on regardless, as he had done in the disastrous Gallipoli campaign thirty years before. The Ju 87 Stuka dive-bombers made the Aegean notorious as the destroyers' graveyard. The only airfield not in German hands was on Cos, far to the north of Rhodes. British troops landed by parachute to secure Cos airfield during the night of 14 September, and a Spitfire squadron flew in next day. Three days later they were joined by more substantial forces carried in by destroyers. When HMS *Petard* joined the campaign in October 1943, the Greek destroyer *Queen Olga*, her companion in many earlier actions, had already been lost; in mid-September she had sunk two German-manned merchant ships carrying troops to the islands, but on 26 September she was bombed by Stukas and sunk with the loss of her captain, Cdr Georges Blessas, and seventy of her crew. Her companion destroyer, HMS *Intrepid*, was also sunk.

At dawn on 3 October German parachutists overwhelmed the company of British troops defending Cos airfield, and 2,000 more German troops landed from 17 ships supported by 130 bombers. The Navy had failed to intercept the ships carrying the German troops because three destroyers had been withdrawn to screen battleships concentrated off Malta. The forced withdrawal of the Spitfires from Cos left Allied shipping at the mercy of the Stukas, and Churchill made desperate pleas to Eisenhower and his British deputy, ACM Sir Arthur Tedder, for air cover during a lull in fighting in Italy. In token response American Lightning fighters were briefly based at El Adem airfield near the Libyan city of Benghazi.

News of the fall of Cos came on 7 October as *Petard* and *Panther*, escorting the anti-aircraft cruiser *Carlisle*, entered the fray. With two other destroyers they searched for a German invasion force reported to be heading for the island of Leros, recently occupied by British troops. They failed to make a sighting before retiring back through the dangerous Scarpento Straits by dawn. The other two destroyers were relieved by the *Rockwood* and the Greek *Miaoulis*, and the five ships returned north through the straits in daylight at 25 knots. All was quiet while American Lightnings patrolled overhead, relieved by others at half-hour intervals. But the sky began to cloud over and the sixth relief flight of Lightnings was overdue when Reg Crang's radio direction-finding hut warned of aircraft approaching. It was thought they had picked up the expected Lightning fighters. Instead, sixteen Stukas came out of the sun. They concentrated on the big vessel, hitting the *Carlisle* amidships with four direct hits, while near misses blew off her starboard propellor and shaft. In a brief lull the *Panther* backed towards the *Carlisle*, intending to take her in tow, when more Stukas arrived.

The *Panther* was just getting up forward speed in order to dodge the bombs when she received two direct hits amidships and two near misses. She was moving at speed and seemed to dive beneath the calm sea. Most of the upper deck crew were picked up by the *Miaoulis* following astern of her. The overdue Lightnings at last arrived, finally locating the ships by spotting the explosions and the smoke of battle. Four Stukas had been shot down by ack-ack fire from the ships, the *Petard*'s 4-in guns firing twenty-two rounds a minute, and the pom-poms and oerlikons firing as fast as their crews could reload. The Lightnings quickly eliminated another ten Stukas and the Ju 88 that had been shadowing the British ships. But their late arrival had cost the Navy a cruiser and a destroyer.

Bridge lookout Mervyn Romeril recalled:

Seeing that we had no air cover the Stukas quickly swarmed around the Carlisle. We were doing large circles around her firing all our guns. The captain lay on his back shouting orders to go hard a'port or starboard as he saw the Stukas begin their dives at us. Once a Stuka pilot started his dive at a target he was unable to alter course, so if a ship can alter course fast enough the bombs miss. It was quite hairy. We were straddled with bombs many times, but none hit us. The Panther was about to take the Carlisle in tow when more Stukas came at us, and she was getting underway when she was hit and disappeared in a cloud of spray. When we came around again I saw only her bows and stern sticking above water so she had broken in half. On our third time round she was gone.

This was the Lightnings' last operation over the Aegean, as Gen Eisenhower's deputy, Tedder, had already ordered their transfer back to the Italian campaign, virtually leaving the Dodecanese campaign without air cover. Two British aircraft carriers and six escort carriers were in the Mediterranean at the time, yet none was diverted to give air cover to the embattled ships in the Aegean.

John Mackness recalled that the Lightnings' intervention was the only time that air cover was really good. 'For the most part the only air cover was provided by Beaufighters from airfields in Cyprus, and because of the distance they could not stay with the ships for long periods. As soon as they left, a Ju 88 would find us and call in the Stukas.' He added,

'The Stuka attacks were worse than anything else we experienced.'

The *Carlisle* was towed back to Alexandria without coming under further attack, having suffered eighteen killed and seventeen wounded, but she was damaged beyond repair.

After that, the *Petard* made two trips to the island of Leros, crowded with troops and decks crammed with vehicles and stores, sheltering in Turkish waters by day and going on in darkness, unsighted by German aircraft. During a third trip she came under heavy air attack by the light of flares without being hit. In Leros harbour she was bombed so heavily that unloading had to be abandoned and *Petard* returned to the open sea, taking troops and some of the equipment back to Alexandria with her.

Petard's fourth run of the Stuka bomber gauntlet was led by the destroyer *Eclipse*, whose captain was Cdr E. Mack. The two destroyers' decks were stacked with Army equipment and soldiers of the East Kent Regiment (the Buffs) crammed into the mess decks. Reg Crang noted on 26 October, 'The situation has become so grave that the destroyer commodore himself went in the Eclipse to assess the situation at first hand.' The *Eclipse*, carrying Cdre Percy Todd, commander of Levant destroyers, and the *Petard*, carrying 188 soldiers of the Buffs below decks, their vehicles and other equipment covering most of the deck space, sailed at dusk on 23 October. They were accompanied by the Hunt class destroyers *Aldenham*, *Exmoor*, *Hursley* and *Rockwood*, with the cruiser *Phoebe* to give ack-ack cover until she turned back at the safety line south of Rhodes, a line laid down by Navy chiefs at the border of areas considered too risky for valuable heavy ships to enter.

Reg Crang's diary told of the following events:

On our way up we received grim news. Most unusually this was given by Aldis lamp signal from a Beaufighter aircraft. The message was that two Hunt class destroyers, the Hurworth and the Greek Adrias, had run into a minefield. The Hurworth sank in burning oil with terrible loss of life, and the Adrias had her bows blown off but the captain still managed to beach the ship. He reported the position of the minefield to the aircraft for transmission to the ships on their way north, but somewhere along the chain of signals a tragic mistake was made in recording the mined area.

This should have been given as east of the island of Kalymnos, but in the received message it was given as west of that island. The Eclipse ordered the remaining Hunt class destroyers to leave the area and create a diversion by bombarding another island. This was to improve the chances of our making a successful unloading at Leros. The Eclipse, followed very closely by the Petard, set a new course to the east of Kalymnos straight into the minefield. She blew up with an appalling explosion no more than 200 yards ahead of us. Within seconds she was gone.

Skipper Egan brought the Petard to stop by an urgent call for full astern both engines. The immediate priority was to find survivors and this task lessened the fear and tension felt by soldiers and crew alike of the terror created by a minefield on a pitch black night. Again the loss of life was quite awful. There were 220 crew on that destroyer and another 200 of the Buffs regiment. Only 44 were picked up by our whalers. Among those killed was Commodore

Percy Todd, ironically on his way to see how bad the situation really was. The captain of the Eclipse, Commander Mack, was saved along with the colonel commanding the Buffs. We learned later that a few strong swimmers managed to reach the mainland of Turkey, an amazing feat.

We now had about 440 men aboard a destroyer designed to carry about 150. We felt really sorry for the soldiers aboard. They were in a far worse plight than we were. This ill-conceived plan to invade a few of the Dodecanese islands was clearly on the way to disaster. The troops could only hope for a quick end to the campaign and then to be taken prisoner. The two remaining Hunts came alongside and took off the troops to disembark them in Alinda Bay. For the moment we were free to leave these desperate waters and steam at high speed for Alex, there to land the fortunate few who survived the tragic end of the Eclipse.

For the *Petard*'s fifth sortie into the Aegean, Lt Cdr Egan was senior officer of a three-destroyer flotilla, all carrying troops and equipment bound for Leros. The cruiser *Aurora* sailed with them, and her more powerful anti-aircraft fire was soon needed. A large formation of Ju 88s, escorted by six Me 109s, bombed from high level, but all their bombs dropped into the sea. One was shot down by the barrage from the four ships.

After more high-level attacks, fourteen Stukas appeared and hit the *Aurora*, putting many of her guns out of action, killing forty-six and wounding twenty. She was escorted away by the destroyer *Beaufort*, leaving *Petard* and *Belvoir* to continue to Leros. Shortly before dusk sixteen Ju 88s attacked, but the two destroyers' evasive tactics during 40 minutes succeeded in avoiding the bombs, and then a Beaufighter arrived and chased the bombers away. Later, another eight Ju 88s dropped their bombs, without result, from high level, but one came back at low level and dropped a bomb on the *Belvoir* just behind her forward gun. It passed through two decks but did not explode. It was manhandled up ladders and dropped over the ship's stern.

Lt Cdr Egan ordered a tactical retreat, still harried by Ju 88s, but turned back in darkness to spend the rest of the night and all the next day in Turkish territorial waters. The following night they reached Leros and disembarked troops and equipment before finding their way back to the Turkish coast. There they were boarded by the local harbour master, who was satisfied with the reason for their presence when he saw an auxiliary engine stripped down for an imaginary fault. He enjoyed the hospitality of the wardroom until darkness fell, and then the two ships sailed through the night to Alexandria.

The *Petard*'s next forays into the Aegean were aimed at heading off German invasion shipping heading towards Leros. Ships believed to be mustered for this had been reported in the area of Kalmynos Island. The first night out RDF picked up a surface craft at two miles, and when searchlights were switched on they spotlighted two small sailing caiques and a landing craft, all brim-full of German troops. *Petard* and *Rockwood* and the Polish destroyer *Krakowiak*, opened up with main armament, setting the ships ablaze.

Soon afterwards, a star-shell fired over Kalmynos harbour revealed a large merchant ship alongside a jetty. Fire from the destroyers set it ablaze, and Lt Cdr Egan took *Petard* right into the mouth of the harbour to confirm that it was destroyed. Then he ordered a torpedo to be fired through the harbour entrance. While passing close by the island of Cos the 4-in gun crews changed from anti-aircraft mode and bombarded aircraft as they were taking off from the runway at Marmari airfield. As the moon rose, swarms of German bombers began attacks lasting hours, some of them flying over the ships in tactics recognised as those used for launching glider bombs. Several of these landed nearby, and just after midnight the *Rockwood* was hit by a bomb which failed to explode. It went through the vessel and out below the waterline, damaging her steering, and while the guns of both ships blasted away, with guns realigned in ack-ack mode, the *Petard* fixed a line and towed the *Rockwood* towards the safety of neutral Turkish waters. Two waves of bombers dropped flares and bombs without effect as they crossed ten miles of open sea to neutral waters. There the bomb hole was patched up and the *Rockwood* was later towed back to Alexandria.

On 12 November the German invasion of Leros began, as the *Petard*'s 4-in guns were being relined by the *Woolwich* depot ship in Alexandria for the second time in a month. Resistance by the ill-equipped British forces taken to Leros at such high cost lasted just five days, the same five days the *Petard* was laid up beside the *Woolwich*. The Leros garrison was overwhelmed by paratroops after being heavily battered by Stukas. Over 3,000 British became prisoners of war with only about 250 escaping to internment in Turkey. Over 5,000 Italians, whose government declared war on Germany the following day, also surrendered. Many Italian officers were shot as turncoats.

On 19 November the *Petard* sailed on her last foray – her eighth – into the dreaded Aegean. Her task was to help evacuate British Army and RAF personnel whom it was thought may have managed to find boats and escape from Leros to hide out on the island of Cos, but no escapees were found.

The costly Dodecanese adventure was over. Apart from the suffering of the Greek islanders, the Italian garrisons newly transformed from enemies to allies, and the British Army and Air Force, the Royal Navy undoubtedly paid the highest price in ships and lives. Six destroyers, two submarines and eight smaller craft were sunk by aircraft or mines, four cruisers and four destroyers were damaged. The Aegean campaign was an example of how the best military intelligence like Ultra was useless without the military means to take advantage of it.

The *Petard*'s sorely tried crew were relieved to hear that they were ordered to Haifa for a boiler clean and crew leave over Christmas. Then the ship joined the escort for the battleships *Queen Elizabeth*, *Valiant* and *Renown*, and the aircraft carriers *Illustrious* and *Unicorn* at Alexandria. The buzz was that the *Petard* would be going east with them to fight the Japanese.

Chapter Seven

Sinking a Japanese Super-submarine

The formidable battle fleet assembled at Alexandria passed through the Suez Canal, escorted by the *Petard* and the destroyers *Paladin*, *Pathfinder* and *Rocket*, in January 1944, bound variously for the Pacific and East Indies Fleet. Soon after arrival at Trincomalee, the Eastern Fleet base on the north-east coast of Ceylon (now Sri Lanka), *Petard* and *Paladin* were ordered to meet five troopships of Convoy KR8 and escort them on the last stage of their voyage from the Kenyan naval base of Kilindini to Colombo. The troopships were carrying African troops to Burma, and a large party of Wrens, ATS and hospital sisters.

The destroyers crossed the equator, with traditional 'crossing the line' ceremonial, to Addu Atoll, south of the Maldive Islands, where the crews enjoyed swimming from picturesque Indian Ocean beaches while their ships were refuelled from a tanker. American cryptanalysts were reading 90 per cent of Japanese signals known as 'Purple', sent on coding machines less sophisticated than the German Enigma, and no Japanese submarines were believed to be in the area.

Reg Crang noted on 9 February that 'Life has been

good this past fortnight or so, more akin to what it must have been like in the peacetime navy.' Three days later *Petard* was back in action.

At first light on Saturday 12 February the destroyers met the convoy and its single escort, the First World War cruiser *Hawkins*. The convoy commodore, in the liner *Khedive Ismail*, was leading with HMS *Hawkins* on his port side, and the *Varsova* to starboard. The other three vessels followed in their wake. *Petard* had taken up a zigzagging position on the starboard quarter of the convoy, *Paladin* on the port quarter. As no Japanese submarines were suspected to be in the area the convoy was maintaining a straight course in order to make faster progress. All the women were aboard the convoy commodore's ship, the *Khedive Ismail*, which had the most comfortable accommodation. More than 600 Africans of a gunnery regiment, with British officers and NCOs and 200 naval personnel, were packed below. Some of the 40 Queen Alexandra Army nurses, 22 Wren signallers, and Kenyan ATS were sunbathing, others were attending a talent concert in the ship's lounge or playing tombola on the after deck.

In the tropical heat of that somnolent afternoon the *Petard*'s officer of the watch, Lt Robert de Pass, recently appointed the ship's First Lieutenant, spotted what he thought was a periscope in the sunlit water between two of the troopships. He told the author from his home in Petworth, Sussex, fifty-five years later, 'I thought I saw a periscope, not an easy thing to be sure about in a sunlit ocean. Anyway, I turned the ship towards the spot and sounded the alarm bells. Seconds later I saw the tracks of torpedoes heading for the troopships, followed quickly by huge explosions. The *Khedive Ismail* sank in minutes, and by that time the captain had taken over.'

As the liner *Khedive Ismail* went down the *Hawkins* flew flag signals, ordering the convoy to scatter, and sounded sirens. The *Paladin* was already dropping depth charges, but the *Petard*'s skipper held back until he got a firm Asdic contact. Both destroyers lowered whalers to pick up survivors and take the rescued to the *Paladin* so that the *Petard* could concentrate on bringing the submarine to action before it could attack other troopships. The *Petard*'s Asdic crew traced the movements of the submarine – clearly a huge one from the Asdic pings – and the *Paladin* paused over the spot where the ship had gone down, to pick up survivors from debris and oil strewn water.

While *Paladin* took aboard some 260 people, only five of them young women, the *Petard* made repeated depth-charge attacks. Its crew watched, fearing for any survivors who might have been swimming in the area of the huge fountains of water the explosions were sending up. Later, when only bodies floated among the wreckage, the *Petard* was forced to blast the waters right over that spot, too, as Asdic traced the submarine lingering underwater there, apparently using survivors as cover.

The *Petard*'s third pattern of twelve depth charges raised a mountain of water close to her stern. Wreckage blown high into the air was still falling back into the sea when the shape of a huge submarine surfaced in a welter of blown compressed air and spray. Behind its conning tower were large chocks for carrying a two-man submarine and forward of it was a large gun of about 5-in calibre. As the *Petard* crew watched figures scramble out of the conning tower to man the gun, and the submarine began to manoeuvre into position to use torpedoes, salvoes from both destroyers fell around it, hitting the casing, the conning tower and the gun. Men on its casing were blown into the sea. More came out in suicidal bids to man the gun as the submarine manoeuvred to avoid the 4-in shells. The gun was quickly knocked out, and the periscope was bent.

While the *Petard*'s captain checked fire and manoeuvred to avoid torpedo attack, Lt de Pass shouted, 'Paladin is going in to ram, sir.' The other destroyer was going at full speed about 1,000 yd off *Petard*'s starboard beam. Egan yelled 'Stop Her.' The *Petard* sounded sirens and signalled 'Negative ram' by bridge signal lamp and flag hoist. *Paladin* responded at once, heeling over far to port, but too late. The drift drove her broadside on to the enemy submarine's hull, and the submarine's port forward hydroplane opened a 15-ft gash in her side. She came to a stop about 800 yd from the submarine which continued under way. She had a 10 degree list to starboard, and was put out of action.

The submarine commander failed to see that one of his attackers was vulnerable, probably because his periscope had been almost shot away, and to blind the enemy further, pom-pom and oerlikons drenched the conning tower in fire. *Petard* closed on the submarine fast, reducing her speed to 18 knots as she passed 10 ft abreast of it as it travelled at about 8 knots, and dropped a pattern of twelve depth charges as she passed ahead of the enemy craft. Giant columns of water blocked out sight of the submarine, but when the sea settled the enemy was still moving ahead, apparently undamaged. The *Petard* made two similar attacks before it became clear that the depth settings could not be set shallow enough to cause critical damage.

The *Petard* drew off to 3,000 yd and fired 4-in

salvoes from all four guns, but the direct-action shells exploded on contact without penetrating the steel hull of the submarine. There had been no armour-piercing shells in the stores at Trincomalee. The cruiser *Hawkins*, which could have destroyed the submarine with one salvo from her 7.5-in guns, was over the horizon shepherding the remaining ships of the convoy.

Torpedo officer, Lt de Pass, was ordered to align the torpedo tubes on the submarine, still under way at 8 knots, and fire them from torpedo sights on the bridge. The standard drill for attacking moving targets was for salvoes of four torpedoes, but Egan thought that since the target was only 1,000 yd away in flat calm and maximum visibility, a single torpedo would do the job. A 21-in 1-ton torpedo was fired from the forward tubes and the watching crew waited the 45 seconds it would take to reach the target. After two minutes of silence it was clear that it had missed. A second torpedo also missed. Gunner (T) S. Leuillette rang the bridge to protest that firing torpedoes singly could only result in loss of the weapon without hitting the target. His advice was ignored. The third and fourth torpedoes, fired singly, also missed. Leuillette shouted up to the bridge to ask permission to take over firing the remaining torpedoes from the controls at the tubes. He was still ignored. Lt de Pass aimed and fired a fifth torpedo, then a sixth, without making a hit. With only one torpedo left in reserve Lt de Pass fired torpedo number seven. The crew waited grimly through 45 seconds, sighing with relief when a huge column of water and flame blotted out the enemy. When the water settled the submarine had vanished. The crew were too numbed to cheer. The agonising torpedo drama had lasted 70 minutes. It was 2½ hours since the submarine had been blown to the surface, and 3 hours and 10 minutes since the *Khedive Ismail* had gone down.

Now *Petard* was able to go to the aid of her stricken sister ship. She went alongside the *Paladin*, whose leaks had been plugged with hammocks, and took aboard all the survivors. Then she towed the crippled destroyer 150 miles to Addu Atoll. The cruiser *Hawkins*, having seen the four remaining ships of Convoy KR8 reach safe waters, rushed to Addu Atoll to pick up the survivors on board the *Petard*.

Petard's captain, newly promoted to the rank of commander, wrote a bland account in his official report, which remained secret for forty years. In his diary account Reg Crang wrote:

Each time we approached the main body of survivors there was renewed contact with the enemy submarine. More depth charges were dropped causing appalling agony to the group of men and women in the water. Whether by accident or design the submarine was taking refuge beneath them. However, it appeared to slink off, and we had to widen the search area. An hour and a half after the *Khedive Ismail* had gone down we began to get anxious. No depth charges had been dropped for some time and our chances were dwindling. In a few hours it would be dark.

I was standing on the Flag Deck looking out over the starboard quarter when in front of my eyes a conning tower emerged, sudden and sinister. Shouts rang out, signalmen went mad, and for a few moments panic reigned. The ship heeled over violently as we turned hard aport. This was a big submarine and no mistake. It seemed to be armour-plated by the way it withstood our gun-fire. Badly damaged she may have been but clearly she was not going to surrender or go down without a fight. She seemed to be trying to get bows on to us to loose one last desperate torpedo attack.

Although our skipper was the senior officer the captain of *Paladin* now decided to take desperate measures himself. Our sister destroyer had backed off in order to work up speed for a full-blooded ramming of the Japanese submarine. As she was making her charge some of our crew were filled with admiration at the sight and cheered her on. *Paladin* sheered away in time to avoid possible self-destruction but too late to escape all damage. The submarine's projecting hydroplane tore a huge gash in the destroyer's belly. *Paladin* heeled over, taking in water and came to a fullstop, out of the action.

It was now up to us. Our captain decided on an unusual, if not desperate, measure himself. He took us perilously close to the submarine so that we could drop depth charges right in its path. These were set to explode at shallow depth so as to cause maximum damage. These explosions caused spectacular eruptions of giant columns of water all around the oncoming submarine. Yet still the vessel ploughed on, seemingly indestructible. There was only one way to finish her off – a torpedo. Only one would be needed, or so we thought. When it was despatched we held our breath and waited, and waited. There was no explosion. It must have missed. To our utter disbelief a second torpedo also missed the target. So did numbers 3, 4, 5 and 6. By that time our spirits had dropped and we became resigned to failure. But torpedo number 7 (only one remained after that) blew it up with a vengeance, a knock-out blow after a fight that had lasted some hours.

We took aboard some 200 survivors, only two Wrens and three Nursing Sisters (out of 76), a few British sailors and soldiers, while the rest were black troops en route to Burma. The survivors told us heart-breaking stories. One Petty Officer said that when the Khedive Ismail was hit he had been standing on deck with his Wren fiancée. She had no life-belt so he gave her his own and pushed her into the water. He swam to safety but she was not seen again. The poor black troops were very frightened and bewildered.

Former LS Ted Saunders told the author recently:

I was told that while we were hunting the Japanese sub the old man (Skipper Egan) said he thought it was likely the sub had returned to the scene of the sinking and was lying beneath survivors. Shortly afterwards we cut through an area where we saw survivors swimming, and dropped a pattern of depth charges. They fell among people who were still alive and swimming. It was awful to see, but necessary.

I have never forgiven those responsible for us not having armour-piercing shells. The Torpedo gunner became so angry because the normal practice of firing four torpedoes in a band was not being followed that he stood on the iron deck shouting up at the skipper, something quite out of order in the Navy, near mutiny. The bridge simply ignored him.

Robert de Pass recollected fifty-five years later, 'I was in charge of the torpedoes, and some people thought

I was making a hash of it. But we got her with my seventh torpedo. None of the crew survived, but we didn't spend much time looking anyway. We had to go to the help of Paladin.'

Among survivors of the *Khedive Ismail* First Officer John Duncan told an inquiry held in Colombo, 'The destroyers, Paladin and Petard lowered boats and began picking up survivors and we all embarked in Paladin. I could see no one else in the water. The destroyer's motor boats kept searching, but no one else was found.'

The Second Officer, Cecil Munday, said, 'I paddled around among the debris and was dragged aboard a lifeboat with six men in it. We were left about 1½ hours before a boat from the Paladin picked us up.'

William Thomson, second radio officer, recalled, 'I was soon able to clamber aboard a small raft. Dotted here and there were small groups of survivors. The two destroyers were dropping depth charges dangerously close to us. While the depth charge attacks went on a whaler and motor launch from the Petard were still looking for survivors, and their occupants were shaken by the force of the underwater explosions.'

The master of the transport vessel *Ekma*, Capt Denis Gun-Cuninghame, said that in taking avoiding action his ship passed through the edge of debris from the *Khedive Ismail* and his crew were appalled at seeing survivors in the water and being unable to help them.

In his book *Fighting Destroyer* the *Petard*'s former gunnery control officer, G.G. Connell, told of Cdr Egan's real-life dilemma in his effort to prevent the submarine sinking other ships of the convoy. He wrote:

It did not need the near frantic calls from look-outs and gun crews that the depth charges would be close to survivors to realise that the captain had allowed for this factor in his agonising decision to attack and prevent the submarine taking refuge under the main concentration of swimmers struggling for their lives.

The ship's company on the upper deck crouched at their actions stations with sick numbness . . . the eight charge pattern seemed to erupt with greater than normal violence, and the underwater detonations struck the hull with shattering impact emphasising the effect it must be having on those who still fought for their lives in the oil covered sea. . . .

Petard ran in for the third attack steaming now through bodies, black and white, all young, men and girls, none alive to be rescued, the depth charges were launched to fall among the still forms floating in the midst of the debris of their ship.

Connell added that when the survivors were transferred to the *Petard* the six women among them could not bear to be parted from the sailors of the *Paladin* 'who risked death from the paralysing crashes of the depth charges when they dived to the rescue. The girls had been hauled out half dead, and like numbers of the survivors they were hostile and afraid while in the Petard, an attitude that added to the sense of failure and despair felt by the ship's company.'

The official casualty list of 1,297, including 72 women, was among the three heaviest losses of life in one ship, during the war. The destroyers picked up 260 survivors. *Petard* escorted many merchant ships, singly and in convoy. This was the only one of its charges lost through the action of an enemy submarine.

The submarine was the *I-27*, 356 ft long (9 ft longer than the *Petard*), weighing 2,198 tons against the

Petard's 1,800 tons; it had a range of 14,000 miles that could take it from Malaya to the coast of France without refuelling. She had already sunk fifteen large ships and damaged two others. Some submarines of the same class also carried a reconnaissance flying boat.

The findings of a Board of Inquiry held in Colombo a week later focused on the convoy commodore's decision to speed up the convoy's arrival by maintaining a straight course instead of normal zigzagging, a measure that made a U-boat's aim much more difficult. The inquiry found that the commanding officer of HMS *Hawkins*, Capt Josselyn, had made an error of judgment in not zigzagging, and that HMS *Petard* was wrong in firing torpedoes singly. There was no mention of depth-charge attacks near survivors in the water.

Asked by the author about suggestions that depth charges were dropped regardless of survivors being in the water seeking rescue, the former First Lieutenant Robert de Pass paused a long time before saying, 'I don't think any depth charges were dropped where survivors might have been in the water. If that had been true it would have been etched in my mind and never forgotten.'

Uneventful escort duties followed until the *Petard* took part in the first major counterattack against Japanese control of the waters of South East Asia. She joined Force 69 commanded by the Commander-in-Chief, Adm Sir James Somerville, comprising three battleships and four cruisers with strong destroyer escorts. The other group, Force 7, comprised a battlecruiser, two aircraft carriers, a cruiser and destroyer escort. The Japanese failed to detect the fleet's approach, and on 19 April carrier planes launched the first attacks.

Reg Crang noted, 'The Japanese Navy stayed in harbour and only three aircraft ventured out against us. All these were shot down by fighters from the carriers. All the ships fired salvoes into the harbour, the dockyards and the nearby air base. The big shots from the battlers screamed over the destroyers as we went in close with our puny guns. These seemed like pop-guns compared to their 15-inch and 16-inch Big Berthas. At the same time carrier-borne aircraft were bombing and strafing oil tanks and other installations, causing huge fires.'

At the end of July orders came for *Petard* to escort a convoy from the Seychelles to Aden and then proceed home to the UK. Passing through the Mediterranean she diverted to help a merchant ship torpedoed by a single plane north of Benghazi. They found a Liberty ship crowded with a deck cargo of lorries with the sea lapping around the wheels. The *Petard* picked up the twenty-six crew from their lifeboat, tried to start towing the ship but had to give up any promise of salvage because the ship's rudder had jammed. She transferred its crew to the tugs when they arrived, and went on to Malta, staying there only two hours to refuel and take on victuals. She made another brief fuel stop at Gibraltar.

HMS *Petard*, bearing forty-nine patches over her wounds, arrived back in Portsmouth on 16 August 1944. PO Reg Crang was among a handful of senior members of the old crew to return to her from leave to supervise specialist equipment being repaired or replaced.

Chapter Eight
The Second Commission

In dry dock the much-battered *Petard* was gutted, new plates were riveted in place of the forty-nine patches, and she was fitted with new twin 4-in guns in B and X positions, to provide stronger anti-aircraft armament against the menace of Japanese kamikaze suicide planes. A new latticework mast carried new radar equipment. Work was still not completed when her new crew passed Nelson's flagship *Victory* to get to *Petard*'s mooring early in January 1945.

By this time the Germans were using their much-improved U-boats fitted with schnorkels and armed with propeller-homing torpedoes. They were launched in a final offensive against shipping in British coastal waters.

On a fine, sunny day, with her new commissioning pennant streaming, *Petard* headed along the south coast on her way to the Scapa Flow naval base. Through the Irish Sea in raging gales the crew were repeatedly called to 'action stations' as Asdics picked up a total of thirteen U-boat echoes. In better weather on the last stretch to Scapa Flow the Asdic cabin picked up a strong U-boat contact and *Petard* crossed and re-crossed the area for three hours. Depth charges were fired, but there was no sign of debris – the schnorkel must have allowed the

submarine to escape at speed. At Scapa Flow *Petard* was
ordered to rendezvous with a returning Russian convoy,
but soon after she left the base the engineer reported
damage to the propeller, apparently caused by her
own depth charges. She diverted to North Shields
on Tyneside to go into dry dock, and was there as
the European war ended. Then *Petard* was ordered
to join the East Indies Fleet based at Trincomalee
in Ceylon. First she sailed to Gourock dockyard
for yet more work, and leaving the Clyde she
sailed past surrendered U-boats berthed side
by side. Crew members wondered whether the
one they had hunted so persistently a few weeks
before was among them. Their crews lounging on their
decks stared back curiously. As a destroyer *Petard*
represented their most deadly adversary. They must have
been feeling desperately miserable at being defeated. On
the other hand, their war was over. The *Petard*'s crew's
war seemed to be just beginning.

Petard went into dry dock again at Alexandria before
passing through the Suez Canal. As she entered the
Indian Ocean the captain told the ship's company
over loudspeakers that they had to be back at full war
alertness again – Japanese submarines might be in the
area.

At Trincomalee ships crammed the huge natural
harbour, anchored in line after line, as far as the eye
could see. It looked as though HMS *Petard* had arrived
in time for something big.

The overseas news broadcasts of the BBC were now
the only source of news, and the bulletins seemed to be
dominated by the postwar settlement in Europe with
little about the Allies' continuing war against Japan.

Then came news of vital interest. In what was to become known as the Potsdam Declaration, America and Britain warned Japan to accept immediate unconditional surrender or face complete destruction. It didn't seem remotely likely that the Japanese would take much notice. War seemed to stretch far into the future.

The British 14th Army had come to see itself as the Forgotten Army during its long jungle battles far from home. Its enormous victory in Burma had been overshadowed by the German collapse in Europe and the sensational revelations that dominated the newspapers and radio in Britain. Few, even in Britain, realised that the British and Indian Armies engaged more Japanese Army units in Burma than the Americans fought during their island-jumping campaign across the Pacific. The 14th Army had first held the Japanese advance on the Indian frontier and then inflicted the greatest defeat on the Japanese Army in its history. The next objective was to avenge the British Army's most shameful surrender and drive the enemy out of Singapore.

Most of the major British warships that had been tied up in the North Atlantic by the threat of the *Tirpitz* were now deployed against Japan, most of them assigned to an impressive British Pacific Fleet operating under the American supremo, Adm Chester Nimitz. The Americans had reached Okinawa in their island-hopping advance, but their navy and the powerful British Pacific Fleet was only just beginning to operate against the Japanese home islands.

Petard was soon off again, heading for a rendezvous under sealed orders to be opened after she sailed.

Signal traffic was heavy and coders sweated long hours over the code manuals. *Petard* headed through sultry August heat to join up with main units of the East Indies Fleet, and the buzz was that she was to support a major landing somewhere in enemy-occupied territory. She was to be point ship in Operation Zipper, a huge invasion armada involving ships crossing thousands of miles to land some 200,000 troops and their supplies on Malayan beaches near Port Swettenham, for the recapture of Singapore. Pocket guides to Malaya and a glossary of useful Malay phrases were handed out. A footnote warned: 'This description of Malaya is written from memories that end with a huge column of smoke rising from the city of Singapore. Our soldiers and civilians were being rounded up to face the horrors of Nippon barbarism. The Japanese occupation will have left its beastly mark and much of what has been said in these pages may have changed.'

As the *Petard* sailed off the Nicobar Islands the BBC news reported that a new type of bomb of immense destruction power had been dropped on the Japanese city of Hiroshima, followed by a commentary saying that the new bomb (developed, it seemed, as a result of scientists at last succeeding in splitting the atom) had unprecedented powers of destruction. Three days later came news of the dropping of a second atomic bomb on Nagasaki and of Russia's entry into the war against Japan with massive attacks on the Japanese in Manchuria. However, the Japanese still seemed to be ignoring the Potsdam Declaration whose promise of total destruction seemed to be in the process of being carried out.

Petard was ordered back to Trincomalee harbour as the BBC announced the hard-to-believe news that the

Japanese had agreed to surrender. There were excited cheers from her crew. Ships still in harbour put up a celebratory fireworks display by firing flares as *Petard* anchored.

The end of the war might have been a rumour so far as routine aboard the *Petard* was concerned. At sea again next day the crew darkened the ship at sunset, kept vigilant submarine watch, radar and Asdic scans and aircraft lookouts. Signals traffic increased and was still encoded. It wasn't until 17 August that the war was officially over. Admiralty General Message 243A arrived in clear (uncoded) form, and the author remembers his hands shaking with excitement as he copied the telegraphists scrawl onto a signal pad for passing to the bridge. It said:

1. HM Government has announced that the Japanese have surrendered.
2. All offensive operations are therefore to cease forthwith.
3. Some time may elapse before the actual instrument of surrender is signed and before it is clear that Japanese forces have received and intend to carry out the instructions of their High Command. Accordingly danger of attack by individual enemy surface craft, U-boats and aircraft may persist for some time to come.

The Japanese in South-east Asia were not at all inclined to accept their Emperor's order to surrender. Gen Seishiro Itagaki, whose command covered Malaya, Sumatra and Java, suppressed all news of the Emperor's decision to accept the Potsdam Declaration for four days. When it was released in Singapore on 20 August officers at the Japanese 7th Army Command, preparing to resist an expected Allied landing somewhere in Malaya, were angry and resentful. They threatened to defy the Emperor's order and carry on fighting. Gen Itagaki personally announced that any Allied ships that tried to land troops would be fired on, and orders to that effect were sent to shore batteries and coastal defences. Singapore radio declared that the Japanese Army was still supreme, and warned that units of the British fleet in the area of the Nicobar Islands would be attacked.

Adm Mountbatten, the Supreme Commander, South-East Asia, decided that Operation Zipper was too far advanced to be stopped, and the D-Day landings would go ahead on 9 September essentially as planned. But preliminary bombardments and air attacks by the major battleships, aircraft carriers and cruisers the *Petard* was escorting were cancelled. They were to have destroyed Japanese bases posing a threat to the entry of the Allied invasion convoys into the narrow waters of the Malacca Strait, the northern approach to Singapore between Malaya and Sumatra.

The American Pacific war supremo, Gen Douglas MacArthur, who had been entrusted with overall command of arrangements for acceptance of the Japanese surrender, decreed that no landings should be made in Japanese-occupied territories until a representative of the Emperor had signed the overall surrender. He was worried that unless it was clearly seen that the Emperor had surrendered, Japanese forces in outlying garrisons might fight on, as indeed they were threatening to do in Singapore.

Since the formal ceremonial surrender would take time to arrange (it took place in Tokyo Bay on

2 September), this meant British ships had to mark time at sea, far from their bases in Ceylon and India. To save fuel the *Petard* anchored for several days in Trinkat Champong Bay in Japanese-occupied Great Nicobar Island. By day the only movement visible ashore was surf on the untrodden beach and steam rising from the dense green jungle; by night smoking was forbidden on deck, and sentries guarded against visits by local inhabitants who were said to be expert marksmen with poison darts and enthusiastic head-collectors. The ships in the bay ranged in size from minesweepers to destroyers – the other destroyers there were the *Tartar* and *Volage* of Britain's 10th Destroyer Flotilla. Some destroyers remained at sea screening the major ships, and later had to return to Trincomalee to refuel.

All crews were at wartime vigilance. Just one week after VJ day *Petard*'s crew had just finished the midday meal of a kind of tinned meat known as 'dog' and dehydrated potatoes, when the second 'yellow' air-raid warning of the day was received; bells clanged to call everybody to action stations. Pom-pom guns, oerlikon machine-guns, and *Petard*'s 4-in guns pointed expectantly skywards, ready to greet visitors from a 'kamikaze' airfield only 200 miles away. After twenty minutes of tense waiting, the 'raiders past' signal was received. The alert was caused by a single Japanese reconnaissance plane which raced away when fighter planes took off from our carriers patrolling nearby.

New orders came after the overall Japanese commander in South-East Asia, FM Count Juichi Terauchi, sent his Chief of Staff, Gen Takazo Numata, from his Saigon headquarters to Rangoon to sign preliminary agreements about the arrangements for surrender. On his return to Saigon Gen Numata broadcast orders forbidding suicide planes and surface craft to make attacks on British shipping.

The *Petard* escorted a ship carrying marines to a Dutch naval base on the island of Sabang, north of Sumatra, where the author stretched his legs ashore for the first time in some three weeks. The Japanese had obviously evacuated in a great hurry. *Petard* crew members who went ashore found charred documents in piles of ashes and bundles of leaflets printed in Indonesian, which appeared to be backing independence. Other souvenirs included fruit labels used as message pads, badges of rank, a matchbox with a label showing a Japanese plane diving down on a Union Jack, a steel helmet left lying around and amid one pile of ashes a scorched Japanese bayonet.

After a few hours *Petard* sailed into the Malacca Strait and anchored off Georgetown, the capital of Penang Island, where marines had already been put ashore. The Japanese commander, Rear Adm Uzumui, had signed the island's surrender aboard the cruiser *Cleopatra*, wearing his British Distinguished Service Cross and Great War victory medal, won as an ally in the First World War.

At first light *Petard* led the *Cleopatra* and the Royal Indian Navy cruiser *Bengal* through a narrow swept channel marked out by three Indian Navy minesweeping flotillas ahead of them. Spotters around *Petard*'s decks and in the crow's nest directed fire from pom-pom guns, oerlikons and rifles at bobbing mines which the sweepers had cut loose. Some exploded in high spouts of water, presumably others sank.

It was a nerve-racking passage. Scuttles, hatches and watertight doors were all closed, and the ship's boats, two whalers and a motor launch, were swung out on davits in case of hitting a mine the spotters failed to see. All the ship's company, except engine room and wireless staff, were ordered to stay on the upper decks wearing lifebelts. Late that afternoon *Petard* forged ahead of the minesweepers at high speed, ignoring the danger of mines, under orders to intercept an enemy vessel. A lookout reported a smudge of smoke ahead, and a strange looking warship hove into view. *Petard*'s crew was at action stations as she raced towards the Japanese destroyer named *Kamikaze*.

As the *Petard* approached it could be seen she was flying a large white ensign above a smaller rising sun flag of Japan, a signal of surrender. We hove to some 20 yd abreast of the enemy. Her upper decks were crowded with stocky figures in green uniforms, and one lone figure stood out in spotless white uniform, carrying a leather dispatch bag. A murmur of hatred began among the *Petard*'s crew as they lined the rail, staring at the enemy, but it was stilled by a crisp order from the captain on the bridge. Then came a moment of panic among the Japanese crew as a shot rang out, but it was only a line being fired across the *Kamikaze*'s bows.

On the *Kamikaze*'s bridge another figure in sparkling white uniform held a megaphone and spoke in perfect English. He said he was sending over charts and two envelopes. One envelope contained a receipt which he would like signed and returned. The enemy request for a receipt was ignored, and as soon as the dispatch bag was securely on board, the *Petard* sailed back to pass it over to the admiral aboard the *Cleopatra*. (One of the author's pictures of this event was subsequently published in the weekly wartime magazine *War Illustrated* and in his book about the war against Japan

Miracle of Deliverance.) After that *Petard* returned to her position behind the minesweepers, and proceeded on through the narrow marked channel, reaching the Singapore roads the next day. The Japanese commander in Singapore, who had threatened to fight on, had been peremptorily brought to heel by the overall Japanese commander in Saigon, and a few days later he boarded the *Cleopatra* to put his signature to the surrender of the 77,000-strong Japanese garrison. *Petard* anchored within sight of the *Cleopatra* for several hours, then sailed back up the swept channel to anchor at the northern end of the strait. There she stayed for five days and nights, a floating buoy, watching convoys pass through, supplementing a depleted larder by scrounging food from passing bigger ships.

The crew cheered when *Petard* lifted anchor during the afternoon of 8 September – the eve of D-Day – and headed south again, this time as point ship leading a huge invasion armada, assembled after long voyages from many ports on the still potentially dangerous final passage to the landing beaches. The early tropic night came as *Petard* headed from the wide gulf of the Penang area into the narrows of the Malacca Strait, shutting out the brooding smudges of enemy-held shores on either side – Malaya to port, Sumatra to starboard – still harbouring the suicide planes and motor boats that might, but for the atomic bomb, have been exacting a high price for this intrusion into waters where no British surface ship had penetrated for some three years.

Through the night searchlights were used to pick out the narrow swept channel down the Malay coast towards Singapore. Behind, the lights of the following ships stretched as far as the eye could see, a remarkable sight in any event, but a matter of wonder as orders to darken the ships had been in force until the night before. The armada stretched back over forty miles, a gathering of four fast and three slow convoys, which had made the ocean crossing from ports in India and Ceylon through monsoon gales. Among them were landing craft that had been chugging slowly across the ocean for weeks. Aboard some of the older landing ship tanks, veterans of landings in North Africa, Italy and France, engineers had to struggle to keep overworked engines functioning. But the water in the Strait was flat calm.

It was still dark when the *Petard* dropped anchor in her bombardment position at the southern end of the landing beaches, with the crew at action stations. Ready to open fire, too, with all their guns ranged on likely Japanese positions, were the cruisers *Nigeria* and *Ceylon*, the destroyers *Paladin*, *Tartar* and *Nubian*, and the Indian Navy sloops *Cauvery* and *Narbada*. The battleship *Nelson* and the French battleship, *Richelieu*, were in reserve with the crews at their massive guns ready to respond at the first sign of resistance.

The first assault landing craft tanks moved towards the beaches as dawn began to break. Planes from our aircraft carriers patrolled overhead as they hit the beaches. Several hours passed before gun crews were stood down, relaxing in the knowledge that the great assault was not being opposed. The *Petard* lay offshore through that long sweltering day, her crew blissfully unaware that the invading forces were having a hard time getting ashore, and that key units were to be stuck on the beaches through the first night. Only later did they hear of the chaos on beaches that were akin to quicksands, and that the great invasion might have been a bloodbath to rival Gallipoli had the Japanese offered resistance.

Late that D-Day afternoon new orders came for the
Petard. She sailed through the massed lines of anchored
ships off the beaches, and led the battleships *Nelson*
and *Richelieu* through the swept channel down the
last part of the Malacca Strait to Singapore. This time
she anchored closer inshore, not far from the landing
jetties, where were berthed the hospital ships that had
sailed with the Zipper fleet to look after the expected
casualties of our invasion. Stretcher parties were taking
aboard the first of the rescued Britons who had survived
Japanese prisons.

Preparations were going on ashore for a formal
ceremony of surrender of the 680,879 enemy forces in
South-East Asia. It was reported later that Mountbatten
used the occasion to announce that the Japanese were
surrendering to superior forces already established
ashore at Port Swettenham. He added, 'When I visited
the beaches yesterday men were landing in an endless
stream. As I speak there are more than 100,000 ashore.
This invasion would have taken place on 9 September
whether the Japanese had resisted or not. I wish to
make this plain – the surrender today is no negotiated
surrender; the Japanese are surrendering to superior
forces now massed here.'

The *Petard*'s crew were not to hear that highly
dubious boast or to take any part in the ceremony, the
ship having been ordered to sail to Hong Kong, but it
was hoped that one watch – the author's – would get to
stretch legs ashore before sailing. But in the afternoon
a disappointing signal was decoded by him, cancelling
orders for Hong Kong. Instead the *Petard* had to sail
with all speed to a rendezvous in the Timor Sea, and
she headed south at her full speed of 36 knots, crossing
the equator the next day without traditional ceremony,

and joined the cruiser *Cumberland* off Tandjongh Priok, the port of Batavia (now Jakarta), capital of the Dutch East Indies (now Indonesia). An Indonesian nationalist movement, armed by the Japanese, was threatening to oppose the landing of Allied forces there.

A Dutch civil affairs chief, who had arrived in the *Cumberland* expecting to set up office as Lieutenant-Governor of the Netherlands East Indies, was forced to stay aboard the *Cumberland* for safety. The most senior ranking of the released British prisoners, Col Laurens van der Post, was acting as liaison officer with his former captors. On van der Post's advice Mountbatten ordered the Japanese Command, whose troops were still guarding Dutch civilian prisoners, to send soldiers into Batavia to maintain order pending the arrival of British troops. Negotiations were going on with the nationalist leader Dr Sukarno, who had declared Indonesia to be an independent republic two days after the Japanese Emperor accepted surrender.

By the time the *Petard* reached the scene Mountbatten had decided to jaw not war with the nationalists, and after making calls at Celebes and Southern Borneo, the ship returned to Trincomalee. She spent three weeks escorting a floating dock at some 6 knots – hardly enough speed to cause a cooling breeze – to its destination in the newly liberated Andaman Islands. Off the coast of southern Burma on her way back to Singapore *Petard* ran into a tornado, heeling over like a yacht as water slushed everywhere below decks. Within minutes of calm returning the entire ship became an aviary. Flocks of birds, most of them beautifully coloured, some tiny, some big, perched all over the decks, festooned the wireless aerials, and scores of them penetrated into the mess decks. There must have been thousands of birds and hundreds of varieties. The crew couldn't move for flapping birds. The ship was a long way from land, yet most of them were obviously jungle birds, perhaps caught up in the typhoon and blown far out to sea before escaping the wind and seeking refuge on the *Petard*. It was a fantastic sight, but slowly they began to fly off homewards, always towards the east where the nearest land lay. The smaller ones stayed longest, the last of them until land was visible on our port side.

At Singapore the *Petard* needed repairs to storm damage, and berthed at a naval dockyard within sight of the causeway linking the island with Johore on the Malayan mainland. A Japanese cruiser, *Myoko*, was moored with her stern blown off after an attack by British midget submarines a few months before. The area was littered with abandoned Japanese tanks, and Japanese soldiers were put to work by one of the *Petard*'s petty officers. When repairs were done *Petard* called at Tandjongh Priok, sailed to Celebes, lingered off the jungle-fringed beaches of Southern Borneo, then returned to Tandjongh Priok to pick up several Indonesian officers, smartly dressed in chocolate-coloured uniforms. Orders were to take them to Padang on the west coast of Sumatra, to persuade local nationalist leaders to cooperate with Allied forces. Landing parties went ashore at three lighthouses, Ujong, Parcei and Lenarg, on the Medawi Islands, and ordered local 'terrorists' to cease intimidating lighthouse keepers. At Parcei the entire population was gathered on the beach to hear a warning from *Petard*'s captain that if they failed to leave the lighthouse alone their village would be burnt down.

Petard returned to Trincomalee for each watch to

spend alternate weeks at No. 56 Rest Camp in the cool
mountains in the centre of Ceylon, and then rushed
at all speed to join a battle waging in the port of
Sourabaya. The crew were called to action stations as
Petard moved up a narrowing channel separating the
Javanese mainland from the large island of Madura.
The few buildings visible on either shore flew the
saffron and white Indonesian flag, but the country
looked totally deserted. As the seaway narrowed to
only a few hundred yards on each side, the crew heard
the boom of naval guns, the crunch of bombs and the
rattle of machine-guns.

Petard anchored close to a Royal Navy cruiser and
several other destroyers off the dockyard with her gun
crews closed up ready for firing. The other ships had
been bombarding positions ashore to cover a landing of
Gurkhas to recover control of the port area, and RAF
Mosquitos and Thunderbolts were still dive-bombing
rebel positions not far inland. Boatloads of grinning
Gurkhas, waving their fearsome-looking kukri knives
with relish, passed close by in boats taking them to the
jetties that seemed to be a front line. Large rebel forces
were just the other side of the quayside. The *Petard*'s
crew had a grandstand view of RAF planes diving low
to bomb and machine-gun beyond the smoke-haze
around the dockyard buildings only a few hundred
yards away. But her gun crews were soon stood down.
The ship had arrived too late to take part in the action,
as further bombardment was ruled out because Allied
troops were in close contact with the rebels.

When fighting had broken out, the commander of
the British forces in the area, Brig A.W.S. Mallaby, and
several of his officers were killed by a mob as they went
under a white flag of truce to talk with rebel leaders.

Mobs also attacked a convoy carrying 200 Dutch civilian internees, killing their escort of Indian Mahratta soldiers and all but 20 women and children. Hence the severe British reaction. The battle ashore continued for about a month. The Indonesians suffered 1,618 dead and over 3,000 wounded.

Allied casualties in Java in the two months after the Japanese surrender, mostly in Sourabaya, were 98 killed, 197 missing, and over 300 wounded. British troops destroyed or captured 15 armoured cars, 47 field guns, 36 anti-aircraft guns, 7 anti-tank guns, 11 mortars, 75 heavy machine-guns, 55 light machine-guns, 794 rifles, 500 miscellaneous firearms and 400 tons of ammunition.

The Japanese also suffered in these murderous disturbances. Altogether about 1,000 Japanese troops were killed – almost the same number they had lost in capturing the whole of the Netherlands East Indies some three years earlier. (Dutch forces were deliberately thwarted in their desire to recover control of a huge colonial empire established by the Dutch East Indies Company, formed in 1603. They were delayed in transporting their own forces by 'shipping shortages' until the SEAC tasks of rescuing prisoners and internees and removing Japanese forces were completed. Then their efforts to reassert their traditionally firm control led to sporadic fighting for another three years before an independent Indonesian republic was finally accepted.)

After only one night in the battle area *Petard* sailed to Tandjongh Priok and took aboard about a hundred Japanese prisoners, bound for a camp on an island off Singapore for eventual return home to Japan. The crew refused any of them access to crowded mess decks, and they had to find space for themselves on the upper deck. They must have had a miserable time as monsoon storms kept the upper decks awash through most of one night. There were jokes about the numbers having diminished overnight.

While in Singapore a signal ordered *Petard* to Saigon, where the French were also having trouble re-establishing their colonial control after the Japanese occupation. But that order was cancelled and *Petard* instead sailed to Calcutta, where she joined the cruiser *Sussex* and the destroyer *Caprice*, in a flag-showing ceremonial visit to India's largest city.

After more chores in the Netherlands East Indies the *Petard* rushed to Bombay in February to help put down a mutiny in the Royal Indian Navy. *Petard* arrived to find the Indian Navy ships flying black flags, signifying surrender to the Royal Navy cruiser *Glasgow* and its escort of two destroyers which had arrived earlier. *Petard* sailed on to Karachi, where a serious clash had taken place against naval mutineers. The crew of the Indian sloop *Hindustan* had resisted a force of British paratroopers, with loss of life on both sides. Again it was all over when *Petard* moored along the jetty from the *Hindustan*, whose guns had been knocked out by artillery fire from the shore. *Petard* returned to Singapore and crossed the equator eight more times on errands in the Netherlands East Indies. She returned to Trincomalee towards the end of March. There the author left the ship, his demob number having come up. Over two months later, as he stood on Portsmouth station in a new demob suit he was surprised to see several members of the *Petard*'s crew. She had just arrived in Portsmouth.

Epilogue

Peace turned rapidly into the decades of the Cold War, but HMS *Petard*'s days of sailing the oceans were over. In September 1946 she was placed in reserve at Harwich, where she remained until April 1953, when her number was changed to D56 in the Chatham reserve. In May 1953 she was sailed to Belfast and converted to Type 36 frigate F26. In 1956 she was mothballed in Southampton and towed to Devonport where she was laid up until 1960, when she was briefly part of the Plymouth squadron. She was recommissioned in Portsmouth from 3 September 1960 until June 1962, then put on the Devonport reserve for five years. Finally, in 1967, she was taken to Bowness to be broken up. By that time she was the last of the P and O boats laid down at the beginning of the Second World War.

However, the Cold War did keep Bletchley Park in business, though the secrets of its work in reading Soviet communications are likely to stay secret much longer, perhaps, than its work during the Second World War.

Although the ability to read many Enigma messages was the main provider of information for Allied intelligence, the Germans remained confident that their Enigma codes remained unbroken throughout the war. This confidence was based on the complexity of the machine and frequent changes and amendments to signals procedure.

The fact that Triton remained virtually unbroken for over ten months shows that radio operators in the U-boats used the Enigma with sufficient care to make Enigma 4 unbreakable. Just as the double encipherment of the message key had enabled the Poles to break into the early Enigma codes, it was inadequate message keys that provided entry into Triton. Bad handling of messages, particularly weather reports, by operators on other German signals networks had provided the Bletchley Park code-breakers with the cribs to break into the earlier Enigma traffic.

A new Enigma, that would have put Bletchley right back to square one, was being prepared for use, but like Doenitz's super-submarines and other German secret weapons, it was already too late.

The Germans had attributed the diversion of convoys away from assembled U-boat wolf-packs to Allied espionage, and believed that the sinking of every supply tanker, as well as Ultra's information on U-boats' positions, was due to a new Allied radar. One thing is certain. No agents could have supplied the high-grade intelligence that was issued from Bletchley, coming as it did from German operational signals.

In his posthumously published autobiography *The Enigma Spy*, a former Bletchley Park translator, John Cairncross, claimed he made an important contribution to Allied victory, by supplying the Russians with Enigma signal intelligence that was a critical factor in the defeat of the German armies at the Battle of Kursk in 1943. He explained that when he joined the German-speaking translators at Bletchley Park in 1942 he had been determined to sever his connections with the KGB, begun as a Cambridge student, and was shocked to be told that Britain's Soviet ally had not been advised of the breaking of the Enigma codes, because if it was leaked to the Germans Bletchley Park might never break a new Enigma code. He thought the sanitised versions of Ultra the Russians were likely to be provided with would be inadequate, and renewed contact with his KGB controller.

He first obtained assurances that the material would be sent from London to Moscow by courier and would never be included in the texts of signals sent within Russia. During his year in Hut 6 he passed the KGB many original German texts of messages intercepted from enemy formations on the Eastern Front; some he translated himself, others he picked up from the floor of Hut 6 where other translators had dropped them. This material enabled the Soviet Air Force to pre-empt a German offensive backed by 2,500 tanks, resulting in Soviet victory in the biggest tank battle in history and the start of the Red Army's march on Berlin. Cairncross revealed that the KGB also received English-language versions or sanitised summaries from an MI 14 analyst who worked on the Wehrmacht's order of battle.

Besides various types of Enigma, the Germans used another cipher machine called the Lorenze which had ten rotors. This was used for high-grade diplomatic traffic to embassies in neutral countries, but also to send Hitler's directives and broad strategic plans to distant commands. Bletchley knew it as 'Fish' and in June 1944 ten giant electronic machines called Colossus were installed to break its system of twelve wheels set in different patterns. The value of the messages it decoded is still kept secret, but it is believed that one of the most important of them was Hitler's directive to Gen Von

Kluge, which led to the decisive Battle of Falaise and the American breakthrough across France.

Because of the tight secrecy surrounding his work Turing's singular contribution to victory was never officially acknowledged before he committed suicide in 1954, although his chief Edward Travis was knighted. Winterbotham also received no special recognition, but he made his name by being the first to break the secret of Bletchley Park's work when he wrote a 1974 best seller entitled *The Ultra Secret*. It told mainly about Ultra's influence in the land and air battles and little about the Navy's use of it. Winterbotham died in 1990.

Occasionally, as in the case of the destroyer captain who sailed his convoy into a waiting U-boat wolf pack, Ultra intelligence was disregarded because its incomparable source was not known below the rank of the top commanders. But it was also ignored by commanders who knew that the source of Ultra was the enemy's own operational signals traffic.

These commanders included Gen Bernard Montgomery, despite the fact that some of the most brilliant Ultra successes were achieved during the campaign in North Africa. Ultra gave details of the routes of Rommel's supply ships, and after a reconnaissance plane was flown to the area to disguise the fact that knowledge of the convoy's whereabouts came from Enigma, they were sunk in large numbers. It was claimed that Montgomery's headquarters were sometimes informed of the contents of messages before Rommel saw them himself. Because of one Montgomery failure to make full use of Ultra, Rommel was able to extract the Afrika Korps from the Alamein area and make a fighting retreat. Ultra's provision of enemy tank numbers and other details showed that Rommel's forces had been so reduced after the Alamein battle that Montgomery could have overwhelmed them had he continued the Eighth Army's advance without pause. The day before the costly blunder at Arnhem in September 1944 a special messenger was sent to Montgomery's headquarters in Brussels with an Ultra message warning that his troops would be parachuting into a hornet's nest. He apparently didn't read the message, and British paratroops landed in an area where two German panzer regiments were camped. The survivors were forced to retreat to Allied lines at Nijmegen.

Adm Lord Louis Mountbatten disregarded at least two Ultra messages during the launching of a huge raid on Dieppe in 1942. He was warned that a heavily armed German naval patrol would be operating in areas off Dieppe on the night the raiders would be approaching. As a result the German patrol boats attacked the landing force at 3.30 a.m. and alerted the Dieppe garrison. The raid by 5,000 Canadian, 1,000 British and 50 US rangers was a tragic failure, with more than half the raiding force killed or captured.

By contrast the American Gen George Patton carried a signals truck with his own command tank and relied heavily on Ultra during his breakout across France from the Normandy bridgehead.

Did Ultra win the war as some have claimed? It would have been won without Ultra because of the rate that America was turning out Liberty ships, but there is no doubt that without Ultra, victory would have come much later and at a much greater cost in lives. Indeed, had the European war continued another year it is likely that Doenitz's super-submarines would have been able to bombard cities in the United States, and Berlin might have been the target of the first atomic bomb.

Ultra was partially instrumental in the decision to withdraw the British Expeditionary Force from the chaos of the French collapse in June 1940, a question of survival. Ultra also had some influence in creating the tactics that won the vital Battle of Britain. It was a key factor in turning the tide on the Eastern Front. The Middle East commander, Gen Harold Alexander, said in Tunisia in 1943: 'The knowledge not only of the enemy's precise strength and disposition but also how, when and where he intends to carry out his operations has brought a new dimension into the prosecution of the war.'

The wartime commander of RAF Coastal Command, Sir John Slessor, wrote in a foreword to Winterbotham's book *The Ultra Secret* in 1974: 'The Admiralty were allowed to keep these signals intelligence matters in their own hands, characteristically and not always with happy results. But I have the best reason to know that in the Battle of the Atlantic Ultra, in conjunction with HF/DF, was a real war winner.'

There is no doubt Ultra played a major part in the defeat of the U-boats that was crucial to British survival and in the build-up of the mighty forces for the re-conquest of western Europe.

The statement by Ralph Erskine in his 1988 Intelligence and National Security report, already referred to, properly sums it up:

Bletchley Park's work on Triton would have been to no avail had it not been for the men at the sharp end of the fighting. Without the bravery of Lieutenant

Anthony Fasson, Able Seaman Colin Grazier and 16-year-old Tommy Brown [Fasson's and Grazier's George Crosses are both on display in the Scottish United Services Museum in Edinburgh Castle. In Grazier's hometown of Tamworth the old police station is being converted to the Colin Grazier Hotel, with plans for an upper lounge named after Anthony Fasson and a ground floor bar named after Tommy Brown], in retrieving the Wetterkurzschlussel and Kurzsignaleft from *U-559* there would have been little or no special intelligence from Triton for the first six crucial months of 1943. Few acts of courage by three individuals can ever have had such far reaching consequences. Without special intelligence from Triton, the U-boats would still have been defeated in the long run, but the cost in human life in the global conflict would have been even more terrible than it was.

Appendix One

The Polish Contribution to Breaking the Enigma

The Enigma coding machine owed its concept to an American named Edward Hebern, who in 1915 devised a machine-generated code by adapting a newly produced electric typewriter. The letter keys of the electric typewriter were switches with each key connected to its appropriate letter. Hebern simply rearranged the wiring so that the letters printed were different to the letters on the keyboard. The letters ADVANCE might be printed BXKBZTJ and with the addition of suitable switching circuits the machine was reversible. Encoding and decoding took no longer than the time to type the message. But messages sent on Hebern's machine, while secure from general readers, offered no difficulty to a cryptanalyst. All Western languages have a characteristic repetition rate of letters, whatever the text, and letter frequency analysis is the cornerstone of cryptanalysis. Realising this, Hebern experimented with a machine using rotors which switched the connections of his electric typewriter each time a key was pressed. He eventually sold what he called an Electric Code Machine (US patent 1,683,072) to the US Navy in 1928.

In Germany, Jugo Koch of Delft developed a secret writing machine he called just that in German: *Geheimschrijfmachine*. He sold the patent rights to Arthur Scherbius, an engineer, who went into production in 1923 with a three-rotor machine he called Enigma. This was exhibited by the German post office at an International Postal Union Congress as an inexpensive, reliable means of safeguarding commercial cables and telegrams. This came to the notice of the *Chiffrierabteilung* (the Cipher Department of the Reichwehr, the small army Germany was permitted under the Versailles Treaty), and its head, Col Erich Fellgiebel, ordered its complete withdrawal from the commercial market.

In Poland, reborn after a century of partition as a result of the Versailles Treaty and surrounded by potential enemies, the highly alert intelligence service Biuro Szyfrow (BS4) was keeping close tabs on Hitler's military preparations. They were concerned that increased German military radio traffic on their border indicated readiness for operations outside Germany, because such internal traffic would normally use landlines. In 1928 their customs delayed a package sent by rail to the German embassy in Warsaw, and called in the experts. It arrived on a Friday evening, and despite diplomatic protests the Polish postal authorities insisted that their offices could not be opened again until Monday morning. Polish intelligences's Fourth Section (BS4) were able to spend the weekend examining a new commercial military Enigma machine before carefully repacking it and making it available to the unsuspecting German embassy.

This provided valuable information about the

internal wiring of the Enigma's three rotors and
an additional plugboard that produced final super-
encipherment. One of their mathematical team,
Marian Rejewski, reconstructed Enigma's wiring
cryptanalytically, and a rare commercial Enigma
they had acquired in Sweden was adapted to military
standards. In 1931 a clerk in the German Defence
Ministry, Hans-Thilo Schmidt (later code-named
Asche) alerted the French security authorities to a new
German coding machine. He approached the French
Service Renseignements (intelligence service) offering
documents relating to what he claimed was the most
closely guarded secret of German intelligence, the
Enigma machine. (After the fall of France Asche was
arrested and shot, after the French agent he had first
met – then an agent of Vichy France – denounced him.)

Up to the outbreak of war Asche made contact with
French intelligence officers nineteen times and gave
them hundreds of photographs of highly classified
German documents. At one meeting in 1932 he handed
over an instruction manual for the Enigma machine
and a sample enciphered message with its plain text
equivalent. These were passed on to Polish intelligence
and with their help and the machine they called the
Bombe, Polish cryptanalysts were reading many
messages sent on the original Enigma machine until
almost the end of 1938.

On 15 December 1938, the Germans issued two
additional rotors for every Enigma machine so that the
three operational rotors were now to be selected from
the set of five. This increased the possible combinations
by a factor of ten, from six to sixty, which meant that
many more Bombes were needed to transcribe Enigma
messages, with many more highly trained staff required

to operate them. This was beyond Polish resources and German Enigma traffic was secure again.

A preliminary meeting between French, Polish and British intelligence officials took place in Paris in January 1939. The Poles invited French and British representatives to a second meeting, which was held in Poland the following 14 July, six weeks before Germany invaded Poland. Three cipher chiefs from Britain met their opposite numbers from France and Poland at the headquarters of the Polish secret Enigma-breaking operation in a pine forest near the village of Pyry, 20 miles south-east of Warsaw. The Polish chief revealed the extent of Polish penetration of Enigma and the problem of the introduction of the additional rotors. It was agreed that there should be a tripartite effort to break the five-rotor cipher. The British undertook to use their greater resources to design and construct at least the sixty Bombes needed if the five-rotor Enigma code was to be broken. The Poles told the British all they knew and gave them plans of the Bombes needed. A month later a Polish AVA copy of an Enigma machine was delivered to London.

Polish mathematicians working on decoding Enigma signals were among the team to escape from Poland ahead of the German Army. They fled to Bucharest and found refuge with the French embassy, moving on to France to join a French team working on breaking the Enigma. They escaped again from the advancing German Army, to unoccupied France, where they continued their work with a clandestine French section called Unit 300, established in the Château Fouzes near Avignon. (They claimed to have broken 673 German signals, mainly about the Afrika Korps, and sent the decrypts by radio to a house in Stanmore manned by Poles who had escaped to London.)

In November 1942 a German column raided the Château Fouzes and found it empty, Unit 300 having been forewarned. Several members were later caught and interrogated by the Gestapo, but while admitting that they had broken the pre-war Enigma, which the Germans had already discovered, they managed to convince their interrogators that the wartime changes had made the later version impregnable. Two of the Polish mathematicians, Marian Rejewski and Henryk Zgalski, escaped across Spain to Gibraltar, from where they were brought to Britain. A third, Jerzy Rozicki, died in a ship torpedoed in the Mediterranean. Members of Unit 300 who reached Britain safely held a reunion party at the White Horse Inn at Boxmoor in Hampshire, near the headquarters of the Polish Army Signals Corps.

Appendix Two
Wartime Destroyers

About 1 in 3 of the 456 destroyers that took part in the war were lost. Aircraft sank 56; of these 27 were lost in the Mediterranean. Submarines took 39 and 27 were sunk by mines; 16 were lost for reasons unrelated to enemy action.

The toll of P class fleet destroyers was higher than average: HMS *Porcupine* was torpedoed in the western Mediterranean on 9 December 1942; HMS *Partridge* was torpedoed west of Oran on 18 December 1942; the flotilla leader HMS *Pakenham* was damaged so heavily in a battle with Italian destroyers on 16 April 1943 that it had to be sunk by a sister destroyer; HMS *Panther* was sunk by bombing off Rhodes on 9 October 1943.

The *Petard*, *Paladin* and *Penn* were still operational when war ended.

Appendix Three
Allied Breaking of Naval Enigma

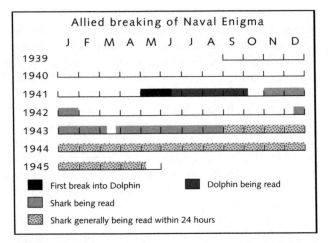

Diagram showing how Enigma materials captured by HMS *Petard* enabled Bletchley Park cryptanalysts to read U-boat signals with some delay from the last weeks of 1942 to August 1943 and to read them consistently within 24 hours for the last 20 months of the war.

Bibliography

Beesly, Patrick, *Very Special Intelligence* (1971).
Cairncross, John, *The Enigma Spy* (1997).
Churchill, Winston, *The Gathering Storm* (1949).
——, *Closing the Ring* (1952).
Connell, G.G., *Fighting Destroyer* (1976).
Coward, B.R., *Battleship at War* (1981).
Crabb, Brian James, *Passage to Destiny* (1997).
Denniston, Robin, *Churchill's Secret War* (1997).
Dyer, M.J., *The P and O Class Fleet Destroyers* (1997).
Erskine, Ralph, *Naval Enigma: The Breaking of Heimisch and Triton* (1988).
——, *The First Naval Decrypts of World War II* (1997).
Grove, Eric, *Great Battles of the Royal Navy* (1995).
Haines, Gregory, *Cruiser at War* (1982).
——, *Destroyer at War* (1982).
Harper, Stephen, *Miracle of Deliverance* (1985).
Harris, Robert, *Enigma, a novel* (1995).
Higgins, Trumbull, *Winston Churchill and the Dardanelles* (1963).
Hinsley, F.H., Thomas, E.H., Ransom, C.F.G., and Knight, R.C., *British Intelligence in the Second World War; Its Influence on Strategy and Operations* (1979–88).
Hinsley, F.H. and Stripp, Alan, *The Code Breakers* (1992).

Hough, Richard, *The Longest Battle* (1986).

Hoyt, Edwin P., *The Death of the U-Boats* (1988).

Hughes, Terry and Costello, John, *The Battle of the Atlantic* (1997).

Johnson, Brian, *The Secret War* (1978).

Kahn, David, *Seizing the Enigma* (1990).

Keegan, John, *The Price of Admiralty* (1988).

Lewin, Ronald, *Ultra Goes to War* (1978).

Mallalieu, J.P.W., *Very Ordinary Seaman* (1943).

Montsarrat, Nicholas, *The Cruel Sea*.

Moorhead, Alan, *Montgomery* (1946).

Patterson, George, *A Spoonful of Rice with Salt* (1993).

Peillard, Leonce, *Sink the Tirpitz* (1968).

Rhodes, James Robert, *Gallipoli* (1965).

Roskill, S.W., *HMS Warspite* (1956).

Schmidt, Heniz Werner, *With Rommel in the Desert* (1951).

Trevor-Roper, H.R., *Hitler's War Directives* (1964).

Tute, Warren, *The True Glory* (1983).

——, *The Reluctant Enemies* (1989).

Van der Post, Laurens, *The Admiral's Baby* (1996).

Van der Vat, Dan, *The Atlantic Campaign* (1988).

Welchman, Gordon, *The Hut Six Story* (1982).

Westcombe, Peter and Gallehawk, John, *Getting Back into Shark* (1997).

Wiggan, Richard, *Hunt the Altmark* (1982).

Winterbotham, F.W., *The Ultra Secret* (1974).

Wright, and Logan, *The Royal Navy in Focus 1940–49* (1990).

Ziegler, Philip, *Mountbatten* (1985).

Index